China Seas to Desert Sands

A medical life in six countries

Jean Goodwin

Onwards and Upwards Publishers
Berkeley House,
11 Nightingale Crescent,
Leatherhead,
Surrey,
KT24 6PD.

www.onwardsandupwards.org

ISBN: 978-1-907509-87-2
Typeface: Sabon LT

About the Author

Jean was born by the sea, on the northern coast of China, where her father was headmaster of a school for English-speaking children. She had a happy childhood, but when Japan entered the Second World War she and her family were imprisoned for three years. Back in England, Jean became a secretary and a nurse, and married Stewart, a doctor who had also been in prison camp in China. They were both committed Christians. In spite of their childhood experiences, they turned away from a settled medical life in England, and overcoming their natural fear of leprosy, worked overseas in leprosy hospitals for ten years.

Two of Jean's children were born overseas, and she brought up her four small children in challenging situations including living on a leprosy island in Hong Kong waters. Expecting to return to Hong Kong, she and her family were diverted to Ethiopia, with its huge leprosy problem, and experienced hyenas outside their house, a snake inside it, a nest of cobras in their garden and rabid dogs nearby! She had the joy of seeing many leprosy patients became fine Christians, including a widow from the deserts of Ethiopia who had been abandoned by her husband.

In England again, Stewart became a microbiologist; but, primarily due to financial considerations, they moved to Perth, Western Australia. There, she was pleased to see her children, in spite of the many changes in their lives, becoming self-confident and independent. After fourteen years, their four children had all left Australia, and Jean and Stewart accepted an invitation to go to the United Arab Emirates. They lived inland on the edge of the desert for six years, and experienced the Gulf War. In her multifaceted life, Jean found God was with her in all her circumstances.

Endorsements

At last here is Jean Goodwin's own record of a kaleidoscope of riveting adventures that begins with her as a nine-year-old girl in the same Japanese prisoner of war camp as Eric Liddell of 'Chariots of Fire' fame. Jean evidently inherited the same global outlook that had earlier impelled her grandfather – one of The Cambridge Seven – to take to the world stage. Joined by her medical husband Stewart, the two of them were to face, and outface, the challenges posed across six countries and several decades. From breathtaking innovations in the treatment of leprosy to revolutions, typhoons and the Gulf War of 1991, let the Goodwins animate and expand the worldview of every one of their readers, as they have mine.

Richard Bewes OBE
Former Rector, All Souls Church, Langham Place

This is a superb book. It needs to be read, marked and inwardly digested. So many of us have become accustomed to a soft discipleship that makes very few serious demands on our lifestyle and very scarcely invades our comfort zone. 'From China Seas to Desert Sands' is humbling, inspiring and challenging. Not only that; it is also movingly and compellingly written. I shall treasure my copy and order many more for my friends.

Jonathan Fletcher
Former Vicar of Emmanuel Church, Wimbledon

This is a thrilling story of God's faithfulness in the life of one woman, beginning with her childhood in a Japanese internment camp in China, where her father was headmaster of a Christian school. The persistent thread of God's faithfulness is traced through her marriage to Stewart and his pioneering medical work initially with leprosy sufferers in Hong Kong but then responding to God's call to serve in many different and challenging parts of the world; and the story of God's faithfulness as she shared in her husband's work and brought up her four children through to retirement years back in England.

Right Revd John Went
Former Bishop of Tewkesbury

Born in China before World War II, Jean was nine years old when she was captured by the Japanese and imprisoned for over three years. Jean has embraced challenges, risks and opportunities all her life because of her Christian faith. The areas where Jean and her husband and children lived in Asia, Africa, Australia and the Middle East have changed rapidly so Jean's impressions of these places are of historical interest. Jean has been remarkably honest about her feelings. It is a wonderful, well-written autobiography and it rings with authenticity. Do make certain you read it.

John W Pearman, MD MSc FRCPA
Adjunct Professor, Curtin University, Perth, Australia

Preface

Over the years, many people, friends and acquaintances have listened to stories from my life and have said, "You must write it down!" or "Have you written it down?" So here it is.

My object has always been to give God the glory for the way He has protected and guided us – me, my husband and our four children. I want to encourage others to experience God's leading and assurance when we are challenged to 'embrace the unexpected'.

Living in a country is quite different from paying a brief visit. Making a home means meeting local people and finding out about their culture. We always tried to understand and get on with local people. We came to know their good characteristics – and those that are not so good, as found in all cultures.

During the writing of this book, many memories have been brought back. But through it all I have been reassured and had many useful suggestions from my friend Katharine Makower. I very much appreciate all her support.

My husband, Stewart, has provided enormous help and encouragement from the moment this book about our life was conceived. His knowledge and skill in editing and computing has been vital. My very grateful thanks go to him for all he has done.

Of course, I must also mention our supportive family of four, who have 'survived' the twists and turns of our life together. All have suggested ideas, in particular for the title of the book.

I am indebted to Professor the Lord Ian McColl for his interest and writing his Foreword.

Contents

China Seas to Desert Sands

Jean Goodwin

Foreword by Professor the Lord McColl

This is an exceptionally moving and fascinating account of a family of six who graciously adapted to working in four continents over seven decades. It starts with Jean aged nine, captured in China by brutal Japanese soldiers and imprisoned with her family, where she was half-starved, lost much education, and her family life was totally disrupted. Also in the prison camp was Stewart Goodwin, a boy of her age whom she was later to marry. They overcame all these deprivations, and went on to a life of selfless devotion to others.

Jean's parents were Christian workers in China, and the book has evocative references to heroes of the past who also were in China – 'The Cambridge Seven', including Jean's grandfather William Cassels and C T Studd; Hudson Taylor, and Eric Liddell – the hero of the film 'Chariots of Fire'. To many in their prison camp, Eric was an outstanding help and encouragement, but sadly, he died there. Mention is also made of other people in camps whom I knew.

Jean's book starts with the sheer joy of seeing American paratroopers descending from the sky to rescue them and announce the sudden end of the war, which saved thousands of prisoners from their planned execution. She is honest about her feelings about her Japanese captors and the natural difficulties in terms of forgiving them, especially later when visiting Japan with Stewart, who lectured there.

Adapting to school in England was not easy, but they surmounted the problems and both ended up in St Bartholomew's Hospital, Jean in nursing and Stewart in medicine – when I first met him, while I was a medical student at Guy's Hospital. There followed marriage, training in tropical medicine, and a life of devotion in developing countries especially to leprosy patients in India, Hong Kong and Ethiopia, and finally in the Middle East.

This book is an amazing account of how Jean raised four children in some of the most primitive conditions with all the uncertainties and health hazards, adapting and coping with so many unusual customs and foods, and with so little complaining. At the same time, she supported her pioneering husband in his leprosy work, his outstanding research, and lecturing in many countries.

This is a truly inspiring account of a nurse who triumphed over all kinds of adversity, upheld by a vibrant and mature Christian faith.

Professor the Lord McColl
CBE MS FRCS Hon FDS RCS

Jean Goodwin

CHAPTER ONE

In China for thirteen years, including three years of Japanese imprisonment.

orth China 1945, August 17th, 10:00 a.m. Out of a clear blue sky, on a hot August day, a plane appeared and circled low over our prison camp. Once, twice, and then it turned and flew away. It had an American flag painted on its side.

For three long years, Japanese armed soldiers had kept 1500 of us, British citizens and others, in a 'Civilian Internment Camp' surrounded by high stone walls and barbed wire.

I was thirteen years old.

But now the excitement was intense. Rumours had been circulating for days that the war between Japan and the Allied Forces had ended. Our Japanese guards were more hostile.

An hour later the plane flew over us again and circled the camp. To our amazement, seven men with coloured parachutes dropped out of the plane and floated down into the Chinese countryside just outside our camp.

Every able-bodied adult and child charged to the main gate in the barbed wire fence. There was no stopping all 1500 of us, and the armed Japanese guards seemed bewildered. I remember running past one of the guards. He had fear on his face. We pushed the gates open, and we were outside – our first taste of freedom for a very long time! And we greeted the American paratroopers for the heroes they were.

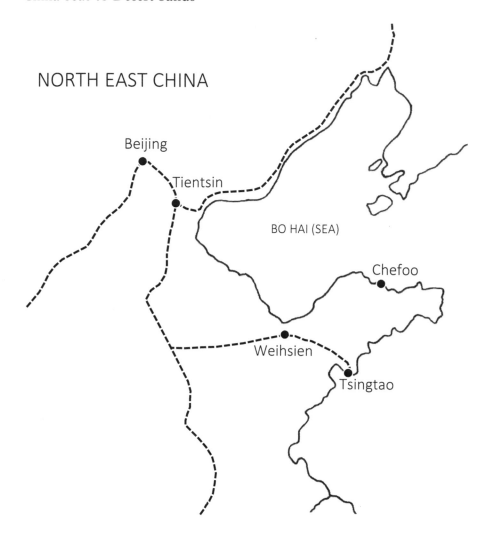

NORTH EAST CHINA

Beijing

Tientsin

BO HAI (SEA)

Chefoo

Weihsien

Tsingtao

My life at Chefoo School, North China

On rising ground, looking out across the sleepy, sun-kissed bay of the port of Chefoo on the North China coast, stood a group of ivy-covered buildings. For nearly fifty years, these buildings had been the home of an English-type boarding school – Chefoo School – where children of Christian workers in the China Inland Mission (CIM) from all over China had received a Bible-oriented, English education. Chefoo School was founded so that the children of CIM staff could go to school in China, rather than living for many years at schools in the 'home' countries away from their parents.

My father, Pat Bruce, was Headmaster from 1930 to 1945, and we lived in our own wing of the main boys school building. Since 1910, my parents had worked in the far west of China with the CIM. After seventeen years in China, my parents resigned from the CIM and returned to England with their five young children (I was not yet born), and bought a house in Gloucestershire. However, after eighteen months happily settled there, my father received a letter from CIM Headquarters asking him to become Headmaster of Chefoo School – much to my mother's horror, I think. After anguished prayer, Pat (and my mother, Jessie) accepted, and Pat toured schools in England and the USA to pick up useful ideas.

In Chefoo, he promoted the best aspects of English education for body, mind and spirit, and was much respected and liked by staff and children alike. He had a great sense of humour. His initials were PA; hence he had the nickname "Pa". As Chefoo (now Yantai) was a major port in the north of China, there were several English businessmen who lived and worked there, and some of their children attended our school – one girl was in my class and became a particular friend of mine.

Chefoo has such a healthy climate that it is now a favoured resort of Chinese government officials. It is very cold in winter with snow and ice, and on one occasion while I lived there, the sea froze for a mile out; and the summers are hot and humid.

I was born in Chefoo in 1932, the sixth child of my parents. My elder brother, Jim, six years older than I, was also in Chefoo while I was there, but my four elder siblings had returned to England. The beaches were safe for bathing, and I learnt to swim at a young age. I loved the huge waves. In the autumn there were fierce storms before the onset of the cooler weather. My cousin Joy, whose parents were working in the middle of China, was two years older than me, and she lived with us in the Headmaster's house.

The school 'compound' was quite large, with paved roads and numerous paths. There were many flowering bushes, blue flax and stands of hollyhocks – great for hide-and-seek. Tamarisk trees and oleander bushes lined the road from the main gate to the school buildings. My mother loved our garden, and flowers grew well there. Our wing of the boys school had wide verandahs and was only a stone's throw from the beach.

I had a Chinese nanny (known as an 'amah') to care for me, to whom I was devoted. She spoke to me in Chinese – in the main Mandarin dialect of China. We also had an excellent Chinese cook, who produced wonderful Chinese meals for us. We had a manservant, who gave me my supper when I came home from school. My parents had a formal meal later each evening, often with visitors. I had a cat, which had kittens in the linen cupboard! And we had a canary.

Chefoo was in a fruit-growing area, and in the spring there was an explosion of pink and white blossom before the pears and apples appeared. Inland, behind the town, there were hills with great walks and places to explore. At weekends, we would take picnics to the waterfalls with climbs over the rocks. Occasionally, a Chinese funeral would pass by with everyone in white (the Chinese colour for mourning), wailing 'music', and paper money impaled on sticks for the afterlife – or a wedding with the bride carried in a 'sedan chair', clothed in red, the Chinese colour of celebration. It was a happy place.

CIM workers would stay in China for four or five years, and then return to their home countries for one year. In 1936, my parents, Jim and I returned to England on the Trans-Siberian Railway across Russia for home leave, before returning to China. It is a very long train journey and took several days, and at stations on the way food and drinks could be bought. I have one vivid memory when my father could not get hot water quickly and the train started to pull out of the station. Fortunately he was a very fast runner, and he just managed to jump onto the end of the train, holding thermos flasks of hot water! I remember I lost my ball out of our compartment, as it went down the corridor, and I never found it. Finally, we arrived by boat in Harwich.

We rented a house and had a 'home life' in England for two years until 1938. It was important to catch up with our family and visit relatives. I had my first experience of nursery school. After eighteen months, Dad left to go on a trip to the USA to visit schools, and then he travelled across the Pacific to China. My mother, Jim and I went back to China by ship via the Suez Canal – a six-week journey. We stopped at Port Said – a fascinating port in Egypt – where we bartered for 'pomelo' fruit over the rails of the ship and watched small boys diving from little boats into the sea for the coins thrown overboard.

In 1936, Japan had begun their brutal invasion and occupation of the whole of Eastern China (including Chefoo). Their massacres and the sexual violence the Japanese soldiers inflicted on thousands of Chinese women are still remembered vividly in China today.

After Japanese gunboats entered Chefoo harbour, stocky little Japanese soldiers in olive green uniforms and heavy boots strutted through the city. Sandbag pillboxes were erected on street and beach and hilltop. At times, trucks crammed with armed Japanese troops roared past the school gates to do battle with Chinese forces in the mountains. Increasing numbers of Chefoo children were unable to get home for the holidays because of widespread fighting between Chinese and Japanese forces, and the difficulties of travelling.

However, in 1939, at the start of the Second World War in Europe, Japan did not join Germany to go to war with England. So British people in China remained 'neutrals', free to come and go as they chose.

7th December 1941 – the day that changed everything for me

This was the day that, in a surprise military strike, the Japanese Navy with 350 bombers attacked the United States naval and air base of Pearl Harbour in the Hawaiian islands of Western USA, sinking battleships and cruisers, and killing and wounding thousands of American sailors and airmen. The USA immediately declared war on Japan; and on the same day the Japanese bombed British-ruled Singapore and Malaya. Britain and the Commonwealth also declared war on Japan, which was now with Germany at war with the Allied Forces including the USA. We were no longer neutral spectators in a Sino-Japanese war. We were 'enemy aliens'.

That evening we listened to the radio for the last time in China and to an English voice saying, "This is London calling in the overseas service of the British Broadcasting Corporation. Here is the news..."

For us in the Far East the date was December 8th, and into our Chefoo School compound marched Japanese officers and soldiers. They posted guards at our gates and told us we were confined to the school area and could go into the town of Chefoo only with their permission. We were each given armbands showing our nationality. Life was extremely frustrating; having always been able to cross the road from our school compound onto the beach and into the sea, now we never went swimming. We were only allowed out of the gate of the compound for short walks if we wore our armbands and with permission by the Japanese guard at the gate. Japanese soldiers made themselves felt, and those on guard duty on our main gate used to practise their bayoneting on sacks of straw hung from wooden cross beams, with bloodcurdling yells. They searched every building and smashed every radio and camera they found.

My father, as Headmaster of the school, together with leading businessmen in the port of Chefoo, was imprisoned and questioned for several weeks. I was nine years old when Japanese soldiers marched into our house shouting for Dad. He, of course, was out teaching, and so my mother had to send for him. I remember that my mother never panicked when things were bad; she was always calm – outwardly at least. The Japanese officers demanded drinks, but our manservant hated the Japanese for what they had done to his country, and he almost refused to serve them.[1] I can remember being alternatively angry and frightened at the invasion of my home. Even now, feelings of animosity against the Japanese remain when I hear Japanese voices, despite all my prayers and good intentions.

The Japanese meanwhile went into Dad's study and started to rummage through everything, looking for incriminating evidence as they suspected he could have been a spy. Dad arrived and they told him they were now taking him away for questioning. It was a horrible moment. When they were gone, my mother sent word around the compound as to the situation, and immediately prayers for Dad's safety ascended to God. Later, the officers returned and walked round our home sticking labels on all the furniture, on things they wanted. When they had gone, Jim and I went round and removed all the stickers. In our garden, there were big dugout pits to keep potted plants during the cold winter months, free from ice and snow. My brother and I persuaded one of the Japanese guards that there was a radio down there. As soon as the soldier went down to investigate, we slammed the lid shut and ran away very fast!

---

[1] During the following months all our Chinese servants left us because we had no money to pay them.

My father and the leading men of Chefoo were imprisoned in Astor House Hotel for questioning. My mother and I walked past the hotel daily to see if we could see anything, and wondered what was happening. I had a pair of red gloves that I would wave like a flag and give the victory sign. It was a most unpleasant experience for the men as they were often beaten, and one man eventually died.

After the war, Dad wrote a description of one of these interrogation sessions:

> On the table lay a big thick cudgel. I was asked why I had gone both to Japan and to England in recent years. The idea was that there must have been some 'Report' on what I had seen in Japan that I had given to the British Government. I said that there'd been none at all.
>
> "Why then did you go back to England?"
>
> I said, "You Japanese are noted for the way you love children. Can't you give us credit for doing the same? My four eldest children are in England..."

My brother Jim was always incorrigibly enterprising and brave. He wrote of how, on a rainy day when the guards were sheltering inside their guard-hut, he managed to get out of the School Compound on a bicycle and cycled past the hotel where my father was imprisoned:

> As I cycled past the Astor House Hotel, I noticed that the sentry had disappeared, obviously sheltering from the rain and spray. Curious about my father's 'prison', I did a U-turn, dismounted and wheeled my bike up to the tall iron railings. I looked up at the broad balconies on the second storey with their iron balustrades. With breath-taking suddenness an idea flashed through my mind.
>
> I looked quickly all round. There was no one in sight. I leaned my bike against the railings and gripped them firmly. Slight and agile at fifteen, it was only seconds before I was standing on the saddle of my bike. Confidently, I looked up. No problem. Eagerly, I grasped the spikes which topped the railings and stepped up on to the top horizontal, reaching up again to grab the balustrade of the balcony. A moment later I was swinging a leg over.

Excitedly, I walked to the windows and saw British faces. I tapped on the pane. Dad appeared, looking tiny (he was 5' 4") at the side of the tall figure of Mr. Bob MacMullan, a local businessman. We smiled at each other and shouted greetings through the firmly-sealed windows. I could hardly hear what he was saying, but soon it became clear he was worried lest a sentry should appear. I took the hint gladly, conscious of the same worry, waved a cheerful farewell and quickly descended by the same route.

I wheeled the bike away, mounted, and in seconds was clear of the danger zone, breathing a sigh of relief but chuckling to myself with schoolboyish glee over the success of this totally unpremeditated exploit. I told my mother, whose instinctive alarm at the potential danger was overshadowed by her spontaneous pleasure in the thought that I'd actually seen Dad and that he was cheerful and well. A few days later a letter to Mother, from Dad, was smuggled out of the prison. There was a special message for me:

"Thank you for coming to see me. I am proud of the courage and initiative you showed. Well done. But if you were caught there'd be consequences for us as well as you. So don't try it again. It's not worth the risk..."

I was so glad to have seen him.

Christmas came, and we were very glad that Dad was allowed out for Christmas. It was a very moving occasion as the whole school, staff and students lined the road from the entrance gate of the compound to welcome him back – such was the love and respect in which he was held. However, he had to return after the holiday for a few further weeks. I was so proud of my Dad that day. Christmas without him would have been dreadful. The fact that he had to return to prison was very hard. Six weeks later all but one of the prisoners were released. The exception was the tall, blunt, ultra-British Bob MacMullan, who seldom bothered to conceal his contempt for the Japanese. He was kept in more than one prison in Chefoo and elsewhere, and died in captivity. Evidence which emerged later pointed towards poison as the cause of death.

Prisoners of War – into a 'Civilian Internment Camp'

During the first few months of 1942, the USA Government arranged for most of their nationals in China to be repatriated by ship back across the Pacific, in exchange for Japanese men in the USA. So the American children and staff left us. By October 1942, the Japanese decided they wanted our Chefoo compound, and on November 5th they marched the whole school through the town up to two walled compounds, each with ordinary houses where European families had lived, on Temple Hill. We were allowed to take only two suitcases each. All the beautiful Chinese things that my parents had acquired had to be left behind, and we never saw them again.

My future husband, Stewart, was also a boy in Chefoo School. He remembers taking the school gong, which used to announce mealtimes; and as we were marched to Temple Hill, with bemused Chinese lining the streets, he banged it loudly while staff and students sang a Christian song that started, "God is still on the throne..."

The girls school – girls and teachers – was put in one small compound, and the boys school and the prep (junior) school in the other. So sixty boys and staff, including my parents and I, lived and slept in a house designed for a family of four people – somewhat cramped. My cousin and I slept on the verandah of the house under mosquito nets. At night, we could hear gunfire from Japanese soldiers fighting Chinese forces in the hills behind Chefoo. Of course we were not allowed out of these small compounds, but amazingly our Japanese Commandant was a Christian and he allowed Dad to visit the girls school under escort almost every day.

We had to stand outside morning and evening for roll-call, counting off in Japanese numbers, to ensure no one had escaped. Numbers one and two in the Japanese language are 'itchi' and 'nee'. One of the boys promptly decided that the numbers three and four should be "scratchy flea"! We all got the giggles, much to the annoyance of the guards, who of course did not understand the joke.

On more than one occasion my brother Jim, typically, managed to escape for a few hours out of our Temple Hill Camp. The first occasion was the on the first day we arrived, as he has described:

On the day of arrival some of the teachers in the Boys' Camp discovered that we were desperately short of electric light bulbs. Two of us senior boys had brought our bikes with us, so we were given a suitcase and hurriedly sent back on a mission to collect some precious light bulbs from the empty buildings before it was too late. These were to be our last moments of lawful freedom for nearly three years, and our last bike ride till the war was over. We pedalled fast and furiously all the way across town, back to the abandoned school buildings, uncertain as to whether we'd be intercepted and ordered back to camp, uncertain as to what we'd find in the old compound. The sentries at the main gate looked astonished as we rode back into the compound, but they said nothing and made no move to stop us. The huge boys school building stood empty and silent. The Japs hadn't yet begun to move in. Good. Uninterrupted we went from room to room through the deserted building, unscrewing light bulbs and placing them in our suitcase ... As we cycled towards the main gate the sentry stepped forward and barred the way. He pointed at the suitcase. "Shemor tsi lito?"[2] he demanded. Robin Hoyte, my companion, remained calm and unflustered. "Dungshi!"[3] he replied innocently. The sentry hesitated, uncertain as to whether he should insist on inspecting the contents. He decided not to interfere, stepped back and waved us through the iron gates. We rode away. We were the last two Chefusians to see that fine old building with its ivy-covered walls. After the war it was looted and burnt, and reduced to a shell. Later the ruins were demolished. The remaining buildings – the whole compound and a substantial area around it – are now part of a large Chinese naval base.

In Temple Hill, getting enough food was difficult and became an increasing problem; but the staff always managed somehow, including killing a pig with much squealing and blood. Mealtimes were impossibly cramped and noisy, and so eventually Dad decided to read during this time – books like John Buchan – so mealtimes became more peaceful. Life was not easy at Temple Hill; lessons were a battle, and everyone had to have a job to help round the houses. That winter was very cold and the summer very hot. In the very limited grounds around the houses there was no opportunity for

---

[2] Japanese for "What's in there?"
[3] Mandarin Chinese for "Things!"

organised games of any sort, which was very hard on sixty active boys; but a move was on the way.

September 1943

At this time the Japanese decided to bring all the foreign nationals under their control in north China to a compound in the middle of Shandong province just outside the city of Weihsien. So all of us in Chefoo were to be transported by ship to the port of Tsingtao and then by train to Weihsien – what a journey! As we were leaving Chefoo, a Chinese baker had to hire a small boat to chase us and drew alongside the ship to pass over the bread that we needed. We slept on boards down in the hold – very airless. We were glad to arrive in Tsingtao and were then put on a train to Weihsien. From the train station, we were herded onto trucks to travel to the 'Civil Assembly Centre Internment Camp' in the country outside the town. We drove through the gates of the camp that were guarded by Japanese soldiers, through the barbed wire fence, but with no welcome from the residents already there, just silence. The people were not expecting schoolchildren, but wanted able-bodied people to help with all the work that had to be done in the camp. It was not a happy beginning for tired and travel-weary youngsters and adults, but this was to be our 'home' for the next two years.

Having been confined since December 1941, firstly for nearly a year in our school compound and then for the last ten months in two houses in Temple Hill, a further two years in Weihsien Camp was a big chunk out of our childhood. The buildings had been built as a seminary for Chinese students, and the compound was about one square mile in size. Double lines of barbed wire with sentry posts were along the walls, and Japanese soldiers patrolled the perimeter night and day. Again, we had roll-call morning and evening to make sure no one had escaped, standing outside in the hot summer and, worse, in the very cold, snowy winters. We soon got to know the soldiers who were reasonable and those who were definitely not pleasant.

It was, we soon discovered, a very cosmopolitan camp. British internees outnumbered all the others put together, but several Commonwealth countries (Canada, Australia, New Zealand and South Africa) were represented, and there was an American minority.

In all there were about a dozen nationalities, including Dutch, Belgian, Greek, Russian and (later in the war) Italian. A wide variety of professions, jobs and skills were also represented. There were top business executives from many commercial firms, and engineers, importers, salesmen and bank clerks. There was a large number of Christian 'missionaries' – Roman Catholic priests and nuns, and every variety of Protestant denomination and tradition. There were professors, lecturers and language students from Chinese colleges and universities; 'White Russians' whose parents had lost everything in their flight east from the 1917 Communist Revolution; four African-Americans, bandsmen from a nightclub in the port of Tientsin; internees of mixed race, half-Chinese, half-Japanese, half-Filipino; drop-outs and hippies; drug addicts, prostitutes, alcoholics and currency smugglers. One eccentric Bulgarian 'conman' – nicknamed "the vulgar Bulgar" – escaped internment for a time through the possession of four different passports, but the Japanese caught up with him eventually.

All our internal arrangements were organised by a committee of the senior businessmen who had been working in North China when war broke out. Ted Mclaren, North China Manager of the large trading company 'Butterfield and Swire', was the Chairman of the Discipline Committee and the leading light of the Council-of-Nine. This wise, honourable, quietly-spoken business chief was the most respected man in the camp and the epitome of personal integrity. He seldom raised his voice, and he was the nearest image to 'the strong, silent Englishman' of fiction, notwithstanding his Scottish ancestry. He met the Japanese commandant regularly.

We Chefoo school pupils and staff were allocated to live in a multi-storey block, and I was in a dormitory with eleven other girls. We did have lessons of a sort but only sitting on our beds and with very little in the way of paper and pencils. It is amazing that any education occurred. Because we grew out of our shoes (and so were barefoot) in the very hot heat of summer we ran fast from one patch of shade to the next. In the winter, with snow and bleak winds, the heating in our block, which was the camp hospital, was by a coal-burning stove on the bottom floor with pipes running up through the floorboards to each storey. For this stove we had to make 'coal-balls' out of coal dust and water; and in the freezing weather making these balls was agonisingly cold for the hands, to the point of tears. One of my abiding memories is the cold. I still dislike being cold.

Food was in very short supply, so the "same old watery stew" was our daily menu, with whatever there was in the way of meat or vegetables thrown in, as the main meal of the day. At the beginning of the day we usually had 'kaoliang' porridge. This was a rough, red grain, normally fed to cattle. Fortunately it did have some vitamin B in it; but for one or two children it caused diarrhoea. So they could not eat it, and by the end of the war they had marked weakness of their arms and legs from nerve damage (beri-beri) due to vitamin B deficiency. We all became very skinny, and most of us stopped growing. There was an 'Ablution Block', one half for men and one half for women, with a shower once a week at a specific time. For elderly women this was a real ordeal as there was no privacy.

All recreation, games and entertainment required the use of imagination and much improvisation. I remember often just throwing a ball with a friend to and fro, for long periods of time. There were no telephones, no shops, no radios, only a very limited number of books, and of course no TV, DVDs or computers. Unsurprisingly, there were on occasion arguments, quarrels and personality clashes. Strict and straight-laced missionaries didn't always get on with cynical, hard-swearing businessmen. Nerves were frayed, and our diet was often inadequate. Old people were querulous or confused. Young people were bored or frustrated. So occasionally the sparks flew. In general, however, dignity, harmony, self-discipline, good humour and willingness to help a neighbour prevailed to an astonishing degree.

We all fought a never-ending losing battle with the bedbugs which infested our rooms. At intervals, on a fine sunny day, mattresses, blankets, camp-beds, boxes and trunks were carried outside. Every blanket was shaken, every seam, every crack was meticulously searched, and every bug or bug's egg was ruthlessly hunted down and exterminated. Boiling water was poured into every crack of bed or box or wall, and the sun was left to finish the job. For a time there'd be peace; then the tiny, squat, red-brown pests would once more creep out of cracks and holes in walls and floors and renew their nightly feasts. Once more we'd toss and turn and scratch and squash.

In June 1944, two 'internees' escaped: Laurence Tipton and Arthur Hummel. Tipton was a senior business executive, and

Hummel was an English teacher from Peking. Both spoke Chinese. The escape was meticulously planned. Father de Jaegher, a twinkle-eyed, white-haired Belgian priest, helped to mastermind the escape. De Jaegher was a scholar and fluent Chinese speaker who had in the past successfully undertaken several dangerous journeys, sometimes travelling incognito through warring Chinese – Nationalists and Communists. In camp, he quickly established a network of agents among the Chinese labourers who came daily to remove the sewage from the camp (we only had 'cesspits'). Through these Chinese he smuggled secret messages in and out of camp, and made contact with local Chinese soldiers in the hills nearby, fighting the Japanese.

The escape was timed to be on a night with a full moon, to assist subsequent progress across the country; also at a time when a dark shadow would cover a suitable stretch of wall; and at changeover time between two shifts of watchtower guards. The two men, dressed in black pyjamas, climbed safely over the electrified barbed wire. After walking or cycling for the rest of the night and all next day, they were welcomed at the fortified village where General Wang of the Chinese Nationalists army had his H.Q.

Mr Mclaren knew of the planned escape, and roll call numbers were 'fixed' the next morning. After the escapees had been given ample time to get clean away, Mclaren then safeguarded the interests of the rest of the camp and the Council-of-Nine by reporting the escape to the Japanese authorities. The Commandant and Police Commander were furious. Troops were sent out to scour the countryside – with no result – and internees in the same dormitories as Tipton and Hummel were arrested and interrogated. But after about ten days they were released back into camp.

To deter any further escape attempts the Japanese surrounded much of the camp with an enormous trench about ten feet deep and about five feet wide. Beyond this trench they erected a second set of high electrified barbed wire entanglements. They reasoned, probably correctly, that this new barrier would not only deter further escape attempts but also discourage any local group of Chinese soldiers from attempting to liberate the camp, or bandits who might kidnap the internees. The rooms of Tipton and Hummel had been on the upper floors of the hospital, the tallest building of the camp, situated near the perimeter. The Japanese suspected that there had been signalling from the hospital to Chinese contacts outside. So all the internees on the two top floors were moved elsewhere. The children and some staff of the Chefoo School took their place. At first the Japanese proposed that all the windows on these floors should be permanently blacked out or blocked up. But Dad, as Headmaster, personally guaranteed that there'd be no escapes by Chefoo School personnel. Thankfully the idea of a black-out was dropped.

My brother Jim described his reaction to the escape:

> *I shared a tiny room, about twelve feet by six feet, on the top floor with three other senior boys. Two camp-beds would just fit in end to end along each wall, leaving a narrow gangway down the middle. There was a small window from which, at times, I would gaze out across the Chinese countryside and yearn for freedom.*

However, my brother was not the only one to gaze out across the countryside and yearn for freedom. Being so constricted was horrid. I still dislike being 'shut in' anywhere.

Jim, at sixteen in the summer of 1942, would have finished his schooling at Chefoo. In the normal course of events he would have left China and returned to England for further education and university; but due to the outbreak of war and the Japanese invasion, this was impossible. It was a particularly difficult time for him and teenagers of his age, confined behind barbed wire with none of the normal facilities for education or entertainment of any sort for the duration of the war. Everyone in the camp, particularly men aged sixteen and older, had to do a job, such as cooking in the large camp kitchen. One of the Chefoo boys was tragically electrocuted after he touched a low electric wire.

Eric Liddell of 'Chariots of Fire' fame was interned with us. His Canadian wife and child had returned to Canada. He was much admired and loved, and was always helping people, whether it was one of the sick and elderly, or a schoolboy needing to repair a battered tennis racquet or hockey stick. There was so little to do in camp that the boys had started playing hockey games on Sunday as well as other days of the week. (Where did they get the energy?) Eric was happy to umpire on weekdays but not on Sundays. However, when the Sunday games degenerated into fights, he offered to umpire on Sundays as well. This was a notable sacrifice, for the sake of the boys, of his life-long principles about Sundays.

In our camp was a so-called witch, with whom very few would associate. She needed help to put up curtains and shelves in her tiny room, and it was only Eric who was prepared to wield a hammer for her. We had a day of Field Sports organised on a patch of ground that we used for games including hockey, American softball, races or jumps. But with Eric Liddell there, it was obviously the track race that everyone wanted to see. There was great excitement, a real buzz and then a hush. It was only a short race, but Eric's head went back (typically) as he approached the line, and of course he won. Yet to my delight, my father, who was also a good sportsman, was close behind him. I was so thrilled! A few months before the end of the war Eric developed a brain tumour and died, and the whole camp mourned. He was buried on the outskirts of the camp, and all those who could, attended the funeral – such a sad occasion.

There were, fortunately, a number of so-called 'war experts' in the camp who gave regular semi-secret briefings or lectures to small groups of internees on the progress of the war. These lecturers had access to the occasional nuggets of hard news, which came in from 'over the wall' by De Jaegher's clandestine methods, often from Tipton and Hummel. Also, by careful analysis of the propaganda of Japanese newspapers and exciting rumours from Chinese traders via the Black Market, they were able to piece together a reasonably accurate idea of how the war was progressing. These war-news sessions, announced only by word of mouth and in some cases protected by a lookout system, were now becoming splendid boosts for our morale. The increasingly rosy tidings of steady Allied advances, both in Europe and in the Pacific, were as 'draughts' of sparkling champagne, enlivening our increasingly grey, chore-bound prison existence. We needed such encouragement as 1945 began.

We now had passed our third internment camp Christmas, and morale was beginning to deteriorate. Official food supplies for the camp kitchens were shrinking. Bread porridge, bread puddings and bread-everything were now standard, but sometimes the flour ran out so there were days without even bread. Because there was no milk, we all had to eat a daily spoonful of 'calcium' in the form of dry, tasteless powdered eggshells. Many of those who carried out the

heavy manual labour in kitchen, bakery and elsewhere were now
steadily losing weight. Incipient malnutrition had begun. There were
cases of dysentery, typhoid and malaria. Internees were now
physically and mentally tired, bored, frustrated and generally run
down as they waited for the war to end. Some internees were stealing
food and coal from communal stocks, risking the public humiliation
of having their names posted on the Camp Notice Board by the
Discipline Committee and, as convicted offenders, having their camp
privileges suspended.

Then one day a string of donkeys laden with boxes ambled into
camp; Red Cross parcels had arrived. It was to us an incredible,
fantastic sight – as if some Aladdin had rubbed his magic lamp and
hit the jackpot. Here was a great table of long-forgotten luxuries
literally being spread before us "in the presence of our enemies"[4] – tin
after tin of milk, coffee, butter, sugar, jam, spam, peaches, salmon,
cheese, chocolate, raisins, cigarettes... Hunger was temporarily
appeased and our morale soared. We learnt later that such parcels
had been sent regularly but had never arrived. They were taken by the
Japanese Army for their own use. In the summer of 1945 rumours
began that the end of the war was near. The guards became very
jittery and we all had a feeling of expectation.

Finally August 17th, 1945 arrived, and as I described at the
beginning of this chapter, we were free! Off to find the parachutists.
Out in the fields, the seven armed, tense Americans were startled to
find themselves being frenziedly hugged and kissed, and their hands
wrung again and again. They were hoisted high on willing shoulders
and borne in triumph to the camp. The guards saluted, somewhat
hesitantly, and bowed low. The American Major returned the salutes
punctiliously from his lofty perch then slid to the ground. "Maybe
you were thrilled to see us," the Major said later, "but you'll never
know how thrilled we were to see you... We descended... guns ready
to shoot it out..." An old lady ran up to the Major and kissed his
hand. He blushed a deep red but did not rebuff her. Carefully he
checked his two pistols and then strode firmly into the office of the
Commandant. To our great surprise the Japanese Commandant
immediately surrendered. In fact, in China there were one million

[4] See Psalm 23 in the Bible

27

Japanese soldiers, and they had never lost a battle. These Americans were very brave men, and we gave them a hero's welcome. All of them had volunteered for this mission. One of them, Jimmy Moore, had been a student at Chefoo School with my dad ('Pa' Bruce). Jimmy Moore respected my dad very much and was determined to make sure Dad and the rest of us from Chefoo were rescued from the Japanese as soon as possible. His first question when he saw us Chefoo kids was, "Where is Pa Bruce? I want to shake his hand." That really made the day for the school!

During the weeks that followed, more Americans flew in using a local airbase. Parachute food drops were a real excitement; we had not seen chocolate for years. During one drop, a small Chinese boy was hit by a container and sustained head injuries. He was taken to our small camp hospital and cared for. Many people prayed for his recovery, and thankfully he was restored to health. The Americans brought us papers and magazines telling of the terrible sufferings of Allied soldiers (USA and British Commonwealth) who had been in prisoner of war camps in Japan, Thailand, Taiwan, etc. We heard after the war that the Commander-in-Chief of the whole Japanese Army throughout the Far East had ordered that at the moment when the first non-Japanese foot landed on Japanese soil, all prisoners in the hands of their soldiers – including civilians – should be immediately killed. After the war, we met English soldiers who had been prisoners in the Far East. They had been made to dig their own graves, to be ready when this order came. However, the two atom bombs came before there was any invasion of Japanese land. The bombs caused terrible suffering, but it meant that Japan surrendered and our lives were saved!

During the war, in the area outside Weihsien Camp there had been fierce fighting between rival Chinese armed groups (Communists and Nationalists), and this continued. So we had to remain in camp until we could be escorted by train to the port of Tsingtao on the coast. At night we would often be woken by gunfire. To wake up on a dark night to the sound of gunfire was scary, not knowing the situation; but then I felt reassured on hearing the American voices of the patrolling soldiers outside my window. The railway line to Tsingtao was constantly being blown up by the Communists, and miles of rail removed. We were very frustrated by delays.

Eventually, the US Colonel Commanding managed to negotiate a ceasefire so we internees could be evacuated. A day was set for the first batch of six hundred to leave. All the Chefoo School party were in this group. We boarded our train, plastered with large Chinese 'characters' proclaiming our identity, and settled down to watch the landscape glide slowly past our windows. In the fields and villages enthusiastic farmers waved and clapped. At every railway station groups of people, banners and slogans hailed the Allied victory.

At Tsingtao, huge crowds massed at the station and thronged the streets to welcome us with flags and applause. The mayor of Tsingtao presented each of us with a small gift. The band of the ship H.M.S. Bermuda played military music, and her captain came forward to welcome us in the name of the British Government. We were whisked off by bus to the 'Edgewater Mansions', a luxury hotel on the bay commandeered for us by the American authorities. That evening, our feet sank into plush carpets as we entered the spacious dining hall. We were ushered to seats in front of gleaming white tablecloths and sparkling cutlery. Attentive waiters served juicy steaks and luscious pork chops, and a jazz band played, inevitably, 'Don't fence me in'. We had one marvellous afternoon on H.M.S. Bermuda, when we were entertained by the marines, shown over the ship and treated to a splendid tea-party.

Since December 1941, my father, my mother and other members of the Chefoo School staff had had very heavy responsibilities for the welfare of all the pupils, aged six to sixteen, separated from their parents and subject to the horrible conditions of internment. These years had taken a heavy toll on all concerned. Jim noted that during all the terrible time in captivity, he had never heard our father grumble once. That remark, to me, spoke volumes about the sort of person my father was, and his resilience; his Christian faith was very real. Due to the prayers of many, and my dad's leadership, it was a very remarkable achievement that every Chefoo student (especially the young girls) was brought out of captivity unharmed physically, except the boy who had died when he had touched a live electric wire; but many suffered severe psychological problems due to prolonged separation from their parents. Also, the examination written papers for the English Oxford and Cambridge University entrance that Dad had carefully supervised were brought by him back to England and accepted by the universities.

In due course we left Tsingtao on an American troopship and journeyed down the coast of China past Shanghai to Hong Kong. The food was good but much too rich for us after our meagre diet for three years. So, as you can imagine, some of the food did not stay in our stomachs. On our journey we passed through the end of a typhoon, which made the sea very rough, and the ship rolled alarmingly. We were glad to reach Hong Kong, where we were handed over to the care of the British forces there. Hong Kong was in a sorry state after the years of Japanese occupation; but to us it was freedom, and we could explore.

Colonel Mike Percival-Price was Commander of the British forces in Hong Kong at the time, and he was married to one of Dad's nieces. He was kindness itself and took us on picnics around the island in his jeep with his driver, who was a young soldier from an African country. One day the jeep backfired, and I 'jumped a mile', much to the driver's amusement.

During the war my eldest sister had been in England and married a Canadian soldier; and they had gone to live in Canada with two small children – my parents' first grandchildren. We really wanted to see them rather than go with the other British internees, who went on troopships directly back to England via the Suez Canal. Fortunately, Mike was able to arrange for our family to travel by ship to Canada, with a few Canadians. Now, after all these experiences in China, we were leaving. It was in December 1945 that my parents, Jim and I left Hong Kong for Vancouver. We were on a huge cargo ship, the 'Empire Chieftain', with only twenty-four passengers. The ship had arrived in Hong Kong from Australia as the war ended, laden with military equipment and food provisions. The captain and crew thought that they were returning to Australia, but when they found they were sailing for Canada, the only material that they could use as ballast was Hong Kong mud.

Halfway across the Pacific we ran into a severe typhoon. The ship pitched and rolled horribly, and most of the passengers took to their beds. The propeller came out of the water with each pitch, and we felt shudders throughout the ship. I have never seen such huge waves, enormous rollers of green marble flecked with white, taller than the ship. Eventually, the captain took the decision to turn the boat and steam into the wind at slow speed. He was a very experienced seaman, and during the war had been torpedoed and spent many days in an open boat before being rescued. He certainly gave us great confidence, and fortunately after three days the storm subsided. At that time there was a complete rainbow over the sea on the starboard side. It seemed like a promise of safety for us. As we approached Vancouver, we went through a snowstorm. It was very cold, and we had no warm clothes. Vancouver harbour was ablaze with coloured flashing neon lights, something we had never seen. We were quite amazed. We arrived late at night, excited and apprehensive – this was a whole new world.

My brother Jim entitled his private account of our time in internment camps 'Birds in the Fowler's Net'. This phrase was taken from the Bible, Psalm 124:7: "As a bird out of the fowler's net escapes away, so is my soul set free." He ended his account at the time we saw the Vancouver skyline:

> ...a kaleidoscope of colour and flashing lights. It was the final touch of magic. This was our welcome, and these were the lights of freedom. As birds out of the fowler's net we had escaped, and our souls were set free.

In Vancouver, kind Red Cross people met us and accommodated us in their hostel. Breakfast the next morning was a feast to us, and my brother and I just stared; we had never seen such choice. Then we were taken to the clothes store and fitted out with suitable warm garments. My parents were greatly looking forward to seeing their eldest daughter again, her husband whom they had never met, and their first two grandchildren. My brother-in-law Ken, who had grown up in Eastern Canada, had been able to get work at a huge paper and pulp mill in the small port of Powell River on the coast north of Vancouver. We sailed on a ferry from Vancouver and at long last met Mary, Ken and their two children. It was lovely to get to know them after such a long separation. We spent Christmas there, which was a joyous celebration.

Finally it was time for us to leave. We took the ferry back to Vancouver and boarded the Canadian Pacific Railway train which took us to Toronto – several days' journey. The dining car was a revelation to us also. The scenery through the Rockies was wonderful. I remember saying to my mother, "I wish I had a camera." She replied, "You will have to keep the photo in your mind." Then came the prairies and miles of flat land. In Toronto we stayed at the CIM headquarters house. Dad was able to confer with the Canadian CIM leaders, but it was not all meetings. We were taken on a trip to see the Niagara Falls – a never-to-be-forgotten experience. The thunder of the cascade, with a rainbow in the spray, was stunning. Donning oil-skins and going behind the Falls themselves was very wet but quite amazing.

While we were there, we were able to see some of our friends from camp who had rejoined their parents in Toronto. The contrast between how different families handled the reunion was very great. Marjorie, from my class, like all the others had not seen her parents for five years. Her mother was absolutely delighted to have her daughter with her again and was determined to establish a good relationship with her. On the other hand, Ken, also from my class, found that his father had no understanding of what his son had experienced and made no effort, seemingly, to find common ground with his son. I found later in England, for another of my friends, Chris, that she had experienced the same difficulties with her parents. Chris had not seen her parents for six years, but when she arrived on a troopship in Southampton she was not met there by her parents. She got on the 'boat-train' to London, where her father was on the station platform, but he totally failed to recognise her. He actually came up to her and asked, "I have come to meet Chris; do you know where she is?" He did not even recognise his daughter! Perhaps that showed how much our malnutrition and suffering had stunted and changed us. Her mother tried to bridge the gap of years but found it very hard to understand her. In later years Chris fell into depression and died of cancer at a young age. A few other students developed schizophrenia at an early age. Such was the tragedy of many children separated from their parents for so long and under such confinement by the Japanese.

For us in Toronto, we boarded the train to Halifax via Montréal, to embark on the ship to Liverpool. It was still winter, and Halifax remains one of the coldest places in my memory; initially there was no heating on the ship. We were crowded and the sea was rough. My mother was always seasick and took to her bed. My father read

Neville Shute's book 'Pastoral' to her, which I also enjoyed as I popped in and out of their cabin. I was thirteen-and-a-half years old when we finally sailed into English waters and reached Liverpool. My sister Patsy met us at the docks. We were actually back in our homeland! So we went on another train journey, to London – but how dismal post-war England seemed after the affluence of Canada! My sister Edith and her husband Alan met us at King's Cross station in their small car. We drove over Westminster Bridge, and there was Big Ben, but no bright neon lights in war-torn London. We stayed with my sister in Peckham, South-East London until we were 'sorted out' and decisions about our future became clearer.

My Family

My maternal grandfather, William Cassels, came from a family of British wine-importers/exporters in Portugal. He was born in 1858 and went back to England for his education at Repton School then Cambridge University. He became a committed Christian and was ordained as a clergyman in the Church of England. After hearing a talk by Hudson Taylor of the China Inland Mission (CIM), he felt the call of God to go and work in that country. The CIM specialised in working deep in the interior of China, unimaginably far away to most English people.

Six other young Englishmen who had also been at Cambridge, including two who played cricket for England, had a similar 'call'. They all left for China with the CIM as the famous 'Cambridge Seven', leaving by ship from England on February 5th, 1885. William had stickers saying "GOD FIRST" on his luggage. The Seven made newspaper headlines, particularly because to be acceptable to the Chinese in inland China and safe from attacks, they would all have to wear Chinese dress. This was not considered at all suitable for well-bred Englishmen.

William was posted to work in the far west province of Sichuan – now with a population of eighty million. This involved a three-month journey by river-boat from the port of Shanghai up the Yangtze River. At that time there were still large boulders in the middle of the river at various points, and when a boat struck one of these, often many people drowned. My grandfather was asked why he had never had such an accident during his forty years in China. He replied that

33

he had always looked carefully at the eyes of the boat captain. If the captain's pupils were very small, which would have been due to smoking opium, he refused to go on that boat.

He travelled extensively through the province on horseback to many towns and villages, often being away for six months each year. He was much loved by the villagers as he journeyed around. As a result of his ministry, many Chinese became Christians and leaders in the church. In due course my grandfather became the first Bishop of West China. In 1887 he married another missionary, Mary Legg, whom he had originally met in London when he was working in a church there. Their first child, Jessie, (my mother) was the first 'white' baby to be born in West China. She caused much curiosity and interest among the Chinese. As was commonly the practice among the British in China, my mother went back to England for her education, at Sherborne Girls School. After further training, she decided to return to China to help her father. Other children were born, a large group of CIM workers joined the Bishop, and a cathedral was built in Baoning. Just before he was due to retire in 1925, he and his wife died of typhoid fever, and are buried in Baoning. The cathedral was shut during the rule of Mao Tse Dong; but it was thrilling to hear of its reopening in 2005, and two hundred people were baptised in it that day.

When my grandfather died, many tributes were given to his work. The Archbishop of Canterbury, Randall Davidson, wrote:

> *The death of Bishop Cassels removes from among us one of the very foremost Missionaries of our time. The work which he has done is not of a perishable sort, and it must have affected the lives of very large number of people. I have known him ever since his consecration [as a Bishop] some thirty years ago, and have always esteemed my interviews with him as privileges of a very sacred kind. His work has been of the simple straightforward kind, presenting the Gospel of Christ to folk who have never heard. I have again and again been impressed by his quiet unassuming perseverance, and by the power he has shown of what missionary work in its most apostolic form can be.*

Bishop Herbert Molony in 1925 was the Bishop of Ningpo Diocese on the east coast of China, and he wrote:

The Bishop's life was an inspiration to many and to me. It was the farewell meeting of the 'Cambridge Seven' at Cambridge in 1885 that was God's call to me to the foreign field, and I remember after the meeting walking back to College with Mr Cassels. His long period of heroic work in the far West of China is one of the high points in the history of missionary enterprise, and his wise and patient meeting of problems and difficulties has always been a great help, and a steadying and inspiring example to us all.

A Chinese clergyman, Rev. K. C. Yu wrote about my grandparents:

Chinese and foreigners felt the loss as greatly as if their own parents had died. How sad we are. When we, the 9000 Christians of the Diocese, think of the hardships of the forty years which Bishop and Mrs Cassels endured, in order to bring us to birth, we naturally feel overwhelmed with sorrow. When Bishop Cassels began to preach in Baoning the people were self-satisfied and proud, yet he continued to preach. By the Grace of God many were won to the Lord, and became co-workers, and so the work increased.

My paternal grandfather, Samuel Bruce, was born in 1838 and brought up in Northern Ireland. As part of the landed gentry, he learnt to hunt, shoot and fish, and had a busy social life. He proposed marriage to a young lady but was refused. He was most upset and decided to go to the Canadian prairies near the earliest site of Winnipeg and shoot buffalo. While he was there, in a remote Indian area, he saw two white men with rifles molesting an Indian girl. He knew that his rifle was more modern than theirs and halted out of their rifle-range. He shouted to them to stop but they refused. So he said, "If you don't stop, I will shoot." They took no notice and he shot one of them dead. The other ran off. My grandfather took the Indian girl back to her camp and discovered that she was the daughter of the tribal chief in that area. The chief told my grandfather that if his daughter had been molested, his tribe would have taken revenge by killing all the white people in that area. He invited my grandfather to stay overnight. During the evening feast, the chief called his 'wise woman' and asked her to tell my grandfather some of his future. She told him that he would marry and his eldest child would be a girl; his daughter would be an excellent horsewoman and she would never have an accident. This turned out to be true and has gone down in the Bruce annals. After my grandfather returned to Ireland, he married Louisa Colthurst of Blarney House and Castle. They moved to Gloucestershire where in due course he became Deputy High Sheriff.

My father, Patrick, their sixth child, was born at Blarney on the 4th of July 1888, and when Pat was Headmaster at Chefoo he would announce a school holiday because it was his birthday; it also happened to be US Independence Day and many American children were in the school. He was brought up on the large estate of his father and was financially independent all his life, never taking a salary or expenses from the CIM; but wartime investments by his solicitors decimated his personal inheritance.

As a teenager at Cheltenham College he became a Christian as a result of the witness of a school friend. He excelled at sport, in particular cricket and rugby, as he did at Cambridge University. After leaving university he worked among the poor in the East End of London, but answered God's call to be a missionary in China with the China Inland Mission. His father strenuously opposed his decision, challenging him that the Bible said you should obey your parents; but my father answered that you should obey God first.

Just before he sailed for China, Dad was among the spectators waiting to watch the England rugby team trial match – Probables against the Possibles. Suddenly, the England Captain rushed up to him, told him a wing-forward had not arrived, and said, "Pat, please would you play for the Possibles." He scored three tries against the English XV; but he chose to follow God to China rather than bask in the glory that his sporting prowess would have brought.

He went to China in 1910 and worked in Baoning, the far west of China, as a teacher in a Chinese boys school attached to the cathedral of Bishop Cassels. He wooed and won Bishop Cassels' eldest daughter Jessie, and they were married on January 15th, 1915.

CHAPTER TWO

In England – becoming a nurse. Marriage to Stewart, and we commit to Christian leprosy work.

My parents, Jim and I arrived back in England in January 1946. Compared to Canada, and even more so China, everything seemed strange. My mother had been born, been brought up, married and lived in China. As was the custom for Westerners there, she had had servants including a cook who did the grocery shopping; so back in England she had to learn all the rudiments of shopping and cooking. This was not at all easy at her age of fifty-eight. I remember my sister Patsy, who was not a cook, trying to teach us how to make custard.

My paternal grandmother, Louisa, was still alive aged ninety-five, and I was glad to be able to visit her in London. She had survived the Blitz and had been rescued from her house after a bomb blast. She was living in a flat and had her grand piano in pride of place in her living room. She was a very musical lady and an excellent pianist. Much to our delight, she gave us tickets for the Bertram Mills Circus.

My sister Edith and her husband, Alan, were kindness itself in helping us all to adjust after our war-time experiences in China and now becoming acquainted with post-war England. Alan, an ordained minister in the Anglican Church of England, was vicar of a Peckham parish. Edith had a group of young teenage East London girls that she organised into a Youth Group with social evenings. I was invited to one such an evening, and one of the team games was all about money. I was a real liability as money had no meaning for me, and I did not understand pounds, shillings and pence, but a cockney[5] girl took pity on me and helped me. She soon had me initiated into the intricacies of mental arithmetic in English money. I have never forgotten her.

The next hurdle was to find a school. My education was sadly lacking. It was suggested that a school in Dulwich might be a possibility, and I was asked to go for an interview. I was thirteen – shy and small, not having grown much during my years in camp. The school girls I met were twice my size and very 'jolly', and I felt quite intimidated. I was ushered into a study-room to do some exam papers, to identify my educational level. I could not do them and felt terrible. Lunch at the school was a nightmare for me, and when I got back home to my parents, I stated emphatically that I was not going to that school!

Fortunately, I learnt that one of my Chefoo school friends was going to Clarendon Boarding School for girls in Malvern, and I decided that it would suit me. So in the middle of the spring term, 1946, I went there. Initially, the school was in Malvern but then moved to North Wales. Having been accustomed to a co-educational school, missing so much education during the war, then having travelled extensively, I had difficulty settling to study. I found out later that the Headmistress had issued an order before my friend and I had arrived that we should never be asked about our time in China, presuming that it was too horrific for us to describe. However, it had been a vital part of our lives, and one evening near 'lights-out' when we were all in bed, one girl asked me about it – and I talked a lot! My description went on after we were supposed to be quiet, but I think a teacher was outside our door and she was as fascinated to listen as everyone else! I have some good memories of that time, but by 1949, having taken my O-level exams, I was glad to leave.

My sister Patsy was training to be a physiotherapist at St Mary's Hospital, London. She would come and visit us in Peckham when she could, and I was really happy to get to know her again after so many years. We had shared a room together at our home in Chefoo, before she left for England just before the war with Germany started. We arranged to meet in London one day, and she took me to see a Danny

---

[5] From East London

Kaye film. I had not seen many films, and I absolutely loved it. We then had a marvellous tea together. But I never got to know her well before she left for Canada to join my sister Mary and found a physiotherapy job in Vancouver.

In 1946, after returning from China, my father decided to train for the Church of England ministry, so he studied for a year at Wycliffe Hall Theological College, Oxford, and we lived there. I found cycling around and exploring Oxford to be fun. I also learnt to row. After Dad was ordained, he worked as a curate (assistant minister) in Buckinghamshire. This was difficult for such a mature man with all his life-experience.

After curacy for a year, he was appointed as Vicar in Hemingford Grey, which is a scenic village on the River Ouse, not far from Cambridge. I spent many happy hours rowing on the river. Dad and I came home one day with a Welsh Collie puppy. My mother was rather taken aback. The dog loved coming on the river with me and enjoyed swimming. He was also company for my father, who went on his bicycle visiting members of his congregation. We stayed there for three years.

My father insisted that I should spend a year at a Domestic Science College (Home Economics), as I had been brought up in a household with a Chinese cook and servants. My minimal knowledge of household duties obviously needed rectifying. It was an enjoyable year and I made a lifelong friend. Helen was the daughter of a friend of my father who was a vicar of a big London church. She was disabled but became a skilled cook. We always remained in touch wherever we were. Many years later, when I was living in Australia, she came out twice in a wheelchair to stay with us! Then I spent a year at a secretarial college in London, after which I worked as a school secretary in Sevenoaks for two years.

I enjoyed my work, and boyfriends came and went. But two years talking on the phone to people, rather than face-to-face, convinced me I was in the wrong place. So in 1955 I made a change of direction. I applied for, and passed, the entrance examination to train as a nurse at the Royal & Ancient St. Bartholomew's Hospital in the centre of London. My work on the wards at "Barts" was very satisfying. We were often given free theatre tickets, and a group of us would enjoy the music or plays, depending on what was on offer. I graduated as a State Registered Nurse in March 1959.

Of course, holidays featured, and I took the opportunity to explore different English counties. I worked as a member of Christian Holiday Beach Missions for children in Devon and Suffolk, and sailed on the Norfolk Broads with friends. Youth hostelling and hitch-hiking in Scotland with an Australian friend meant I saw more of that country, and I did the same with my cousin in Devon and Cornwall. The coastal paths are such a national treasure. Then Keswick and the Lake District, and visiting relatives in Ireland both North and South.

One of my favourite holiday places is the Scilly Isles. I first went there in 1953 with a friend. We had a wonderful time, including a boat trip to Bishop's Rock Lighthouse. I returned there with another friend at a later date and again many years later with my husband and our daughter Caroline. We explored the different islands and beautiful places.

When Stewart and I first met

Stewart and I first met in the summer of 1940, when he arrived in Chefoo to join the school. We were in the same class, but he was (and is) the clever one. His parents had come from England to China with the Church Missionary Society (CMS). His father was a doctor, and his parents worked in the CMS hospital in the large city of Hangzhou, with its beautiful 'West Lake' – four hours by train inland from Shanghai. When he came to Chefoo School, his parents accompanied him to Shanghai, and from there Chefoo School teachers accompanied the party of children, who had come from all over China for two days by sea to Chefoo. Stewart returned to Hangzhou during the Christmas and summer holidays.

His younger sister Joanna started school with him in the autumn term of 1941. So when the Japanese entered our school on December 6th, 1941, they were made prisoners, as we all were. They also came with us to the Weihsien Camp. However, in December 1943, Stewart and Joanna were fortunate to be escorted from our camp and reunited with their parents, who were interned in Lunghwa Camp on the outskirts of Shanghai. The Japanese Government was expecting Japanese people in the UK and USA to be exchanged for all the remaining children of Chefoo School. However, the Japanese in

China realised that fourteen Chefoo schoolchildren had parents who were held in various camps in Shanghai. So they arranged for these children to be escorted by train down to Shanghai. In fact, the international exchange broke down, and the school remained in Weihsien camp.

After 1943, I did not see Stewart again for several years. He returned to England after the war, and a few years later heard of the Chefoo School Reunions that occurred at Christmas time in London. It was at such a reunion, when we were both about sixteen, that we met again. He always says that he found me glamorously beautiful then – and still does!

We saw each other intermittently after that, including one visit to Repton School during his last year there. Stewart went from Repton to Clare College, Cambridge, studying pre-clinical (medical) subjects. While he was at Cambridge, my father was Vicar of Hemingford Grey, just thirteen miles from Cambridge. So once again we were in contact, and we saw quite a lot of each other during his first year there. In 1954, Stewart started his clinical studies as a medical student at St Bartholomew's Hospital in the centre of London – where I was doing my nursing training. It was a busy life for both of us, but we enjoyed the times we had together – most memorably in the spring of 1957, watching a rugby match and visiting Kew Gardens.

Stewart qualified as a doctor in December 1957 and was then appointed as a House Surgeon at the St Alban's branch of Barts Hospital. During the war, Barts had moved its specialised units to Hill End Hospital in St Albans, and he worked in the Orthopaedic Department. It so happened – fortunately for us again – that at the same time I was also posted to Hill End for nursing training. Springtime arrived and the countryside was beautiful. We spent our off duty times together exploring, walking and talking. It was a God-given opportunity for us, with no interruptions from family and friends – a marvellous opportunity for our friendship to develop and love to blossom – which it did!

I always felt that I would be involved in some sort of overseas Christian work, although it would mean separation from family and friends for years at a time. It was familiar 'territory' for me, as many of my family had worked in China. As the friendship between Stewart and I deepened, we discussed the possibility of working with The

Leprosy Mission (then called The Mission to Lepers), and all that it would involve. The Mission's stated object was "to provide spiritual instruction and temporal relief for leprosy patients and their children". Recent advancements in the medical care of leprosy patients meant that much could be done for them, but they also needed to hear of Jesus and His love.

Our decision to consider doing Christian leprosy work was based on our commitment to our Lord Jesus Christ and his command in the Bible: "Go and make disciples of all nations."[6] We had seen how Chinese people welcomed the good news that forgiveness of sins and peace with God are available through Jesus for everyone in the world.

There were not many doctors and nurses working among leprosy patients; Christians were often the only people helping them. Stewart knew doctors in Africa who were on twenty-four-hour call for all diseases, which meant they had no time to preach the gospel of Jesus. We realised that taking up such a career would mean that we would always have only the minimum financially to live on, but as Christians we knew we could trust Jesus Christ with our lives.

I resolved to find out more about leprosy and realised that my natural fear of the disease would need to be overcome. Leprosy patients are such a vulnerable section of society, with many deformities of hands, feet and face, and live in great poverty and alienation. I prayed that God would give me the reassurance and confidence to treat them as people and not as outcasts.

Stewart's mother kept every letter he (and I) wrote to her. In April 1958 he wrote:

> *Last Thursday I met Jean Bruce, and we went to a Leprosy Mission film at a Young People's Church Club in Islington.*

In May he added:

> *I went to a regional Nurses Christian Fellowship meeting with Jean, and heard Paul Brand (a leprosy hand surgeon in India) speak excellently. Jean and I met him, and he had a long conversation with her.*

---

[6] Matthew 28:19

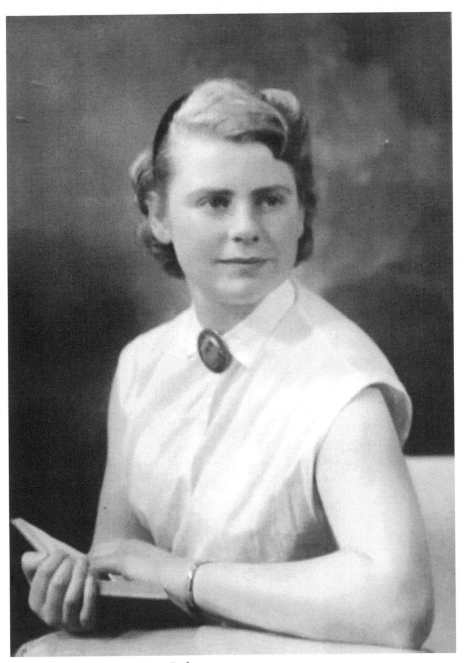

Before our engagement

Stewart learnt as much as he could about leprosy from the Government leprosy specialist Dr Cochrane, who had worked for many years in India, and from Dr Jopling, who was in charge of a small leprosy hospital near Redhill. We learnt that leprosy is a disease that, untreated, develops only slowly, usually over several years, invading the skin and eyes and the nerves in the arms and legs. Since 1947, the drug dapsone, which kills leprosy bacteria, had been given to leprosy patients, but in most patients had to be given for several years.

The earliest sign of leprosy is usually a pale patch of skin – in darker people – and if treatment is given then the disease is halted. However, as leprosy occurs almost exclusively in poor countries and the disease does not cause any pain or fever, patients do not realise that they should come quickly for treatment. Consequently, nerve damage progresses with resulting paralysis of the thumb and fingers, and severe damage to the numb hand and foot. The bacteria may invade the skin of the face and the nose, causing severe disfigurement. Treatment could be given as an outpatient, but many patients, especially those with disfigured faces or hands, were happier to live for months or years in cottages around a leprosy hospital, where they would avoid the social stigma of the disease.

Later, we learnt that many people seem to have an innate resistance to leprosy, so that the bacteria are killed before symptoms develop. In China, among husbands who had leprosy, only five per cent of the wives would show symptoms. Fortunately, it was very uncommon for doctors and nurses working with the patients to show the disease, but of course they all wore white coats and washed their hands.

The Leprosy Mission raised money from Christians in the UK and other countries to cover the expenses of staff from overseas and locally, and the care of patients in their hospitals in countries where leprosy is common. Staff salaries could only be low.

So it was that one day in the middle of May 1958, after we had had a long walk together, Stewart posted his application to become a staff member of The Leprosy Mission. He was accepted later that summer.

It seemed that God had organised our paths to keep crossing – a fact we were very happy with! Stewart invited me to join him and his parents on holiday in Cornwall in the summer of 1958, where we got engaged on July 13th, on a lovely sunny day on a beautiful Cornish headland. In the approved manner, Stewart phoned my father and asked him for his approval – but he did not tell him that he had already asked me! My decision meant I would join Stewart in

working overseas with The Leprosy Mission. This would decide where we lived, possibly for all our working life, and our financial state.

It was the end of my holiday, and I went back to Barts with an engagement ring on my finger, which I couldn't wear 'on duty'.

My final State Nursing exams were looming, at the beginning of 1959, and I had to do some studying. My family were all delighted at our engagement, and for my parents it would be quite a momentous event. They had been unable to attend any other of their children's weddings, due to the separations of the war and living in China. They were not young, and I was the youngest of six in the family. We had decided on a March wedding in 1959 – after my exams – and we all

became very busy. Working in the Operating Theatres, then on Night Duty, as well as studying and wedding preparations, took all my time. We were married just after I took my exams – successfully – and became a State Registered Nurse.

My parents at that time were living in the village of Brenchley in Kent, not far from Tunbridge Wells. It had a charming old Norman church. Interestingly, the Vicar of Brenchley – Dean Trivett – had been Dean of Shanghai Cathedral before the Second World War. He was a Canadian, who had bravely opted to stay in

Shanghai and remain in a Japanese Internment Camp to look after his congregation, while his wife was repatriated back to Canada.

I had two uncles, married to twin sisters of my mother, who had both been bishops in China. Bishop Frank Houghton was also my godfather, and he performed the marriage ceremony for us, with my other uncle and Dean Trivett also taking part in the service. A good friend of Stewart's – a brilliant organist – played for our wedding, coming straight from his job at Eton College to do so. My twin aunts arrived in a hire car from Cheltenham – with their car full of flowers, with which they then decorated our beautiful church. Many family and friends came to help us celebrate our special and wonderful day. We went to the Isle of Wight for our honeymoon, which was also very special and wonderful.

The Leprosy Mission knew that we had both grown up in China and told us that our main destination would be on their leprosy island in Hong Kong waters, where Stewart would be the surgeon. First, he needed to learn the specialised surgery on the hands, feet and eyelids of leprosy patients that had been pioneered by Dr Paul Brand in the city of Vellore, South India. So we would live in India for a year – for six months at the big teaching hospital in Vellore where Paul Brand had his Surgery Unit and then for six months in their specialist leprosy hospital ten miles out in the country. As soon as Stewart had finished his postgraduate medical training in England we could leave.

The Leprosy Mission owned two furnished flats in Kew, used by their overseas workers when they were on leave. Fortunately, one flat was empty in April 1959. So after our honeymoon, we came back to our first home in Kew – just for three months. This enabled Stewart, and to a lesser extent me, to attend lectures at the London Bible College. At that time Stewart began to keep a daily diary.

In July 1959, Stewart started work for six months as House Surgeon at the famous Queen Victoria Plastic Surgery Hospital in East Grinstead. He felt that knowledge of Plastic Surgery procedures would help him correct the facial and other deformities of leprosy patients – and they did indeed benefit from his skill. There were four senior surgeons at East Grinstead including Sir Archibald McIndoe, famous for his skill with pilots, who suffered severe burns during World War II.

I worked in the Outpatient Department there, and so we were able to live in the small married quarters on site. The Outpatient Department was busy and interesting, as eminent physicians, gynaecologists and ophthalmologists from the big London teaching hospitals came to East Grinstead to conduct clinics. However, I was pregnant at this time, and the Outpatient Sister in charge of the clinics was very solicitous of me. When I became obviously pregnant, she suggested that it was time for me to stop working! At East Grinstead, many deformed babies with conditions such as cleft lip and malformed hands were operated on. I found this somewhat disconcerting.

Our baby was due to be born in mid-December, so I could not go on working beyond mid-November. I then went to live with my parents, back in Brenchley, while Stewart finished his six months at East Grinstead. Actually, after a particularly bumpy bus ride, Ruth decided to make an early appearance on December 5th. She was born safely in Redhill Hospital and was baptised by my father in their home on a snowy Sunday, January 10th. All her three godparents were able to be present.

In February 1960, Stewart finished his time at East Grinstead, and we were due to go to India in July. Amazingly, a couple known to a relative in Tunbridge Wells was going to New Zealand for a few months, and allowed Stewart and me and baby Ruth to live in their house near Tunbridge Wells while they were away. It was a spacious bungalow, with a garden of beautiful roses, and came complete with a maid and a gardener, already paid for! It was a tremendous provision for us, just when we needed a home and had no money. Stewart studied Ophthalmology for a few months, which would also be very useful among leprosy patients. Our departure from England was only a few months away!

Stewart's background

Stewart's grandfather, Rev. James Goodwin, worked with CMS in India for seventeen years until 1902. In that year, while he was

47

ferrying food supplies on horseback to starving villagers, he contracted severe malaria and sadly died. He is buried in Bombay. Stewart's father, Dr Theo Goodwin, worked with CMS as an Eye Surgeon in China for sixteen years in Hangzhou, until he and Stewart's mother were imprisoned by the Japanese during the Second World War.

Stewart was born in London in December 1932. At the age of six weeks his parents took him to Hangzhou. His sister, Joanna, was born in 1934. He recounts:

> *My parents read the Bible and prayed with us every day, and from my earliest days I accepted Jesus Christ as my Saviour and have always found Him to be the most wonderful Master and friend.*

In 1936, his family returned to England. In 1937 his father went back alone to work in China, as the Japanese were in Hangzhou, and he was worried for the safety of his wife and small children. But he became dangerously ill with typhus, and Stewart's mother felt she must go to China to nurse him back to health. She left her children with her parents in the beautiful village of Bodiam in Kent, where their grandfather was the minister.

In January 1940, Stewart and his sister went to Canada, where their mother met them. They went across Canada by train and to China by ship. In the summer of 1940, at the age of seven, he went north to be a boarder in Chefoo School. He and his sister were interned in camps with the school until December 1943 and then were moved to join their parents in Lunghwa Camp.

One of Stewart's fellow inmates in Lunghwa was the author J G Ballard, who wrote 'Empire of the Sun' (made into a famous film), which ostensibly describes the camp. As Stewart recorded several times in his secret diary (forbidden by the Japanese), "Played ping-pong[7] with Jamie." In Ballard's final book 'Miracles of Life', he describes Lunghwa Camp in truthful detail and admits that 'Empire of the Sun' was part fiction.

Lunghwa children were fortunate in that they had better schooling conditions than I had in Weihsien, but they seemed to have had less food than we had in our camp. In April 1945, Stewart's diary

---

[7] table tennis

records, "No mid-day meal," and for May 24th, "No breakfast. No supper. Vegetables and gravy for lunch." On a few days their only food was a flat, round piece of baked flour and water, about six inches across. Lunghwa Camp was next to a swampy area with many mosquitoes, and Stewart and his father had repeated attacks of malaria, with no medical treatment available.

For August 16th, 1945, Stewart wrote in his diary, "Got news war has ENDED". As their family home was far away in Hangzhou, they had to remain in Lunghwa Camp, but now with enough food.

Finally, on November 5th, 1945, three years to the day when the Chefoo children were marched by Japanese guards to Temple Hill, the English people were taken on a troopship to England, arriving in December 1945. Stewart's family lived in St Leonards-on-Sea, next to Hastings on the Sussex coast, where his father became a family doctor. Thanks to excellent teachers at his primary school he caught up with his education, in contrast to me. His parents then sent him to boarding school at Repton in Derbyshire in the autumn of 1946, where he stayed for five years. As a committed Christian, his first three years there were miserable, but the situation improved as he became more senior.

While at Clare College, Cambridge he led a children's seaside Christian mission on the Norfolk coast in the summers. At St Bartholomew's Hospital he conducted informal services in the children's ward on Sunday mornings. Owing to an illness of a few months while he was a student, he did not take and pass his exams as a doctor until December 1957, on his 25th birthday. In contrast to all his contemporaries, he was excused military service for two years because he was committed to overseas work.

To India, leprosy work and an unknown future

We were due to leave England for India by ship in July 1960; air travel was far too expensive in those days. All our worldly possessions were packed in three 'trunks' that consisted of a large metal box inside a strong wooden box. Everything was packed for possible rough handling, for example a layer of blanket between each of the dinner plates that we had been given as wedding presents. Ten days before we left, we sent the three trunks to the ship which would sail from Liverpool. We trusted these things would be adequate for our next four years in India and Hong Kong.

Ruth, of course, kept us to a routine of sorts, which was a help. But more importantly, we arranged to see as many friends as possible. We would need their interest and supportive prayer as we coped with challenging situations physically, socially and spiritually, and often in very isolated places. In a letter to all our friends and relatives, we asked them to pray that "the best medical and surgical treatment for leprosy patients will go hand-in-hand with a faithful witness by us to our Lord Jesus Christ". We also sent a card with a photo of the three of us, and underneath the verse, "My food is to do the will of him who sent me, and to finish his work." (John 4:34) Throughout our time overseas, we continued to send 'prayer letters' once or twice every year, and in each chapter I have quoted from them. We were setting forth into an unknown life and work.

CHAPTER THREE

1960-61, in the heat of South India for a year, learning leprosy surgery.

Our departure from England was from Liverpool, on Saturday, July 30th, 1960. The train from London went from Euston Station, where my sister Edith and her son Richard saw us off. It seemed a long journey on the train, but in our compartment was an aristocratic-looking man from Somalia. He told us his name was Abdi Muhammad Jesus, and he was travelling on the same ship as us but getting off in Aden for Somalia. He was glad to talk about Christianity, and on the ship we had some good conversations with him. He accepted a copy of the Gospel of John from us.

At Liverpool, my brother Jim met us and saw us to the ship. As we said goodbye, I shed quite a few tears. Leaving a country by ship feels more like a real farewell than boarding an aeroplane. Passengers line the rails of the ship waving, and those on the docks wave goodbye; finally, land is out of sight. While overseas, we would not easily be able to talk on the telephone, as calls to the Far East were erratic and very expensive. Weekly letters to and from England would be our sole communication.

On the ship – the R.M.S. Cilicia – we were relieved to learn that our trunks had been loaded; but when we found our cabin, we were very dismayed that The Leprosy Mission had booked us into a small cabin for only two people, low down in the ship. The two bunks were so close together that the cot for seven-month-old Ruth had to be jammed between them. We had to climb over her cot to get into our bunks! Also, the ship had no air-conditioning; we would be on the ship for three weeks.

The throbbing of the ship's engines, which was very noticeable in our cabin deeper in the ship, brought to mind our previous journeys to and from China, which we had undertaken earlier in our lives. Also, the showers were salt-water and so soap would not lather.

As we sailed through the Bay of Biscay, we saw Spain on the port side. The next night as we approached Gibraltar, at 1:00 a.m., I crept on deck to see the port, but the ship stopped only to pick up airmail post from England.

On board were other British Christian workers, many returning to work in India, including a Roman Catholic priest who loved talking to us and playing with little Ruth. Stewart suggested to the other Christians that we might have a Bible study, and he was asked to lead a study on the book of Hebrews. Twelve people came, including an Indian and Abdi. One Sunday there was a Christian service on board. We also talked to several Muslim passengers, but they refused to consider that Jesus could be the Son of God. Each day there was an opportunity to play deck-tennis, which Stewart enjoyed very much. Ruth found the movement of the sea very uncomfortable and cried a lot, but she was also teething.

Port Said in Egypt was our first port of call, but the ship only stopped overnight. On sea journeys from China, I had enjoyed stopping here and seeing local people who came in boats alongside, including boys who dived for coins thrown from the ship.

Going by sea through the Suez Canal and the Red Sea in July, in a ship without any air-conditioning, is a very unpleasant experience. The Red Sea is extremely hot and humid at that time of year. We could not sleep in our cabin because it was so hot in the lower decks; but we managed to get some grass mats on deck and slept on them. One small American boy became very ill with the heat. Much prayer went up for him and he did recover after some anxious days for his parents.

As we passed through the Red Sea we saw on the port side the Sinai Peninsula with huge mountains. Aden was our next port, and we were able to go ashore and do some shopping. This made a welcome break. We then sailed across the Indian Ocean, but after the relative calm of the Red Sea, the sea was rough, which made most people feel seasick. Stewart had to stay in his bunk.

In mid-August the ship stopped in Karachi harbour, which was a disaster for us even though we did not go ashore. Hordes of flies descended on the ship, and Ruth developed very severe diarrhoea and fever just before we landed in Bombay on the west coast of India two days later. Ruth's illness lasted for three more days, until after we reached our destination in South-East India, the city of Vellore.

Bombay was, and is, a large and very crowded city – teeming with people. On the docks everything seemed to be moved by hand, with huge numbers of dockworkers. Stewart cleverly managed to locate our trunks among all the others as they were taken off the ship. Customs in Bombay were very kind to us, and we had no duty to pay. We were met by the local representative of The Leprosy Mission, who took us to the Mission guest house in Bombay. On the streets, 'pedicabs'[8] and 'sacred' cows competed for space on the roads with cars, lorries and honking taxes – a cacophony of sound. On the pavements were sophisticated women in their beautiful coloured saris, but also pitiful beggars.

Having lived in China as children, we were accustomed to such large crowds and beggars. However, many years later, when we lived in the Middle East, the impact of India on those who have never experienced it was revealing. At that time, a group of English and American wives of professors travelled to India on a sightseeing visit. None had been there before. One woman was so horrified by the dirt, squalor and deformed beggars outside the hotel that she refused to venture out for the whole of their visit!

We stayed in Bombay for only twenty-four hours. Sadly, as our booking was on a train the next morning, Stewart had no time to visit the grave of his grandfather, who had been buried in Bombay in 1902. It was on August 20th that we left Bombay – fortunately in a 'first class' compartment. Our journey took us two days across India to the east coast, but the journey was not a happy experience, with little Ruth continuing to be very unwell.

On the evening of the second day we arrived in the little station of Katpadi in the state of Madras (now Tamil Nadu). We were met by a wonderful group of people, who would be some of our fellow workers among leprosy patients. They helped us disembark with

---

[8] two-seater vehicles pedalled by a man

Ruth and our trunks. I was especially grateful to a delightful Belgian woman, who took care of Ruth very competently. She was a welcome 'breath of fresh air', wearing a gauzy scarf and perfume – very civilised!

Our 'home' for the next four months was in the staff residential compound of the Christian Medical College (CMC), which was situated on the edge of the city of Vellore. The CMC had been set up for women fifty years earlier by a pioneer American woman doctor, Ida Scudder, as there was no other medical training college for

women in India. By the time we got there, men students were being trained as well.

Our accommodation was in the 'Big Bungalow' - a guest house for the many visitors to the CMC, and a few staff. It was an old-fashioned Indian house of two storeys with a large centre square well, rooms around the well, and a corridor just outside the rooms on each level. Our entire accommodation consisted of one fair-sized room with a small outside verandah and a bathroom, but with only a wire netting door and a thin curtain between us and the rest of the household; so we had minimal privacy!

Ruth, at only eight months old, was unsettled after all the travelling, her recent illness, and her new environment. We were very concerned because when she cried she could be heard by the other people in the house. Later, we learnt that a young American couple who had stayed in that room before us, planning to stay in India for four years, had in fact lasted only six weeks before they had packed up and gone home to the USA! Perhaps our ability to cope with difficult situations came from our childhood experiences in China and our determination to stay the course with our Leprosy Mission work.

At that time, in south India air-conditioning was non-existent. So all the rooms had ceiling fans, and the wire netting door allowed any breeze to flow through from the open windows.

The Head of the CMC was an American who lived alone in the Big Bungalow in a room opposite us. He had his desk there and often worked late in the evenings. When he finished his work, we would often hear him sing a verse of a hymn or chorus. The sound carried clearly through our netting door, and we enjoyed hearing him.

The Big Bungalow was run efficiently by two American women. The Indian senior house servant, Ramasami – with a turban on his head and a smile on his face – was always there to help. The residents and visitors whom we met were a colourful collection of people. An old, unmarried Indian doctor had lived there a long time. During meals he always kept his legs in a cotton bag to avoid being bitten by mosquitoes. A wonderful native Ghanaian, who had come from England to study leprosy work for a few months, was humorous and engaging and was happy to babysit Ruth for us. He caught dengue fever (from a mosquito bite) and experienced the excruciating back pains of this disease. We were very thankful that none of us three caught it.

I employed a young Tamil girl (an 'ayah') for a few hours each day to help me with Ruth. Nappies had to be washed by hand in those days. I was always sad when she would sometimes appear with bruises round her face, undoubtedly caused by her husband. Women in that culture, and especially at that time, were considered very inferior, and the husband could do what he liked with his wife.

Also on the compound was the only Psychiatric Unit for Christian workers in Southern India. Some of these patients joined us for lunch each day. There was one creative but sad lady who was a brilliant pianist. She loved to play the piano for her own relief and played it beautifully – easily heard by us. The meals were always curry of some sort, even on Christmas day. We didn't always appreciate these curries.

There were quite a large number of Indian and non-Indian staff living on the CMC compound. The gardens were extensive with exotic flowering shrubs. Poinsettias flowers were a real feature, and as Christmas approached they turned their gorgeous red colour. I would wander through the gardens with Ruth, and one of her first words on seeing the poinsettias was "pretty" – and they were, giving much pleasure to us all. There were several tennis courts, and in the cooler winter months, we both enjoyed playing tennis with staff friends.

Among the Indian staff was a neurosurgeon. He came from a very high caste (Hindu) Brahmin family in North India and went to England to study to become a neurosurgeon. While he was growing up in India, his father (who was a liberal Hindu) had encouraged him to read the holy books of other religions, including the New Testament of Christians. He was very attracted to the character of Jesus, and when he went to England he met a Christian nurse who told him that anyone could come to Jesus. If they confessed their sin and believed in Him, He would become very real to them as their Saviour. He took this very courageous step, but his family were absolutely horrified. They forced him to undergo electroconvulsive therapy, which usually causes brain damage and is reserved for people with severe depression. However he survived this experience, finished his time in England, and came out to Vellore to continue working as a neurosurgeon. His wife had been instructed to poison him in his food, but she resisted this pressure. He and his wife kindly invited us to their home for tea, and we had many long talks with him. In due course he was appointed the Superintendent of the large Christian Medical College in North West India at Ludhiana. There he would spend time at the weekends preaching on the streets about Jesus.

On one occasion we were invited to have lunch with the female students in their hostel. It was a large dining room, and they all ate with their right hand – no cutlery. In India, and also (as we later discovered) in Ethiopia and in the Middle East, only the right hand is used for eating. At the end of the first course, they went out and washed their hands. The girls wore pretty, coloured saris, especially for any special function such as prize-giving.

The Head of the Leprosy Unit in the CMC Hospital in Vellore was the noted Orthopaedic Surgeon Dr Paul Brand, who was on the staff of The Leprosy Mission. When leprosy causes death of the nerves to the hand, the paralysed fingers and thumb can no longer be straightened. Paul had devised a 'tendon-transfer' operation so that the bent fingers could be straightened and grip again, and another to enable the thumb to move normally. Paralysis of the nerve to the ankle caused 'drop-foot', and Paul had devised an operation so that such patients could walk normally again.

When leprosy patients have lost feeling due to death of the nerves, they can damage their hands without knowing. Nearly all leprosy patients live in poverty and have to do a lot of manual work in the fields and in the home, usually with open fires. So they easily cut and burn themselves, and the wounds can become severely infected and lead to the loss of part of a finger or thumb. Paul's staff taught the patients how to do their daily work without damage to their anaesthetic hands.

In some leprosy patients, the infection inside their nose causes it to collapse. A plastic surgeon in Bombay had pioneered an operation to restore such noses to their normal shape. He visited Vellore while we were there and was happy to show Stewart how he reconstructed these deformed leprosy noses. Later in Hong Kong, Stewart, with his training in plastic surgery, was able to do the same operations.

A bus took the staff every day from the residential compound where we lived to the hospital in the centre of Vellore, about five miles away. Stewart worked in the Leprosy Unit and learnt how to do the operations devised by Dr Brand, including one on leprosy-paralysed eyelids, when a patient could not close their eye. Such paralysis was a disaster, as the eye could easily get damaged, leading to blindness. His days started at 7:30 a.m. and ended at 6:30 p.m. It was a thrilling experience to see a hand like a clenched fist made functional again or a wizened 'old lady' with a sunken nose turning out to be a girl of nineteen a few days later! Stewart enjoyed working with two Indian trainee surgeons – Silas, who came from the far north of India, and Sam – who both were going back to work in Christian leprosy hospitals.

Although the physical state of many leprosy patients could be improved by surgery, many remained with missing fingers and some with blindness and/or deformed faces. The spiritual needs of the patients were left mainly to local ministers, and usually one was on the staff of each Leprosy Mission Hospital; but in our work later in Hong Kong and Ethiopia, we personally took special care to ensure that patients heard the Gospel of Jesus. It was wonderful to see many who accepted Jesus as their Saviour and received miraculously His peace and joy in spite of terrible physical problems. They looked forward to a new and beautiful body in Heaven.

In October, I wrote in a letter:

Probably the most striking impression of life in India is the absolute poverty of most of the people. Women who do the lowest jobs earn just enough each day to pay for rice for two parents and six children. Among the leprosy outpatients, some men were completely destitute, with unkempt hair and only a loincloth. The other great feature of South India is the great heat.

The temperature could reach 42°C (110°F) at the hottest time of the year in April to June, before the rains came. Even in the hospital there was no air-conditioning, only ceiling fans. Because the hospital water pipes went over the roof, the water in them became extremely hot. Leprosy patients in the hospital who had loss of feeling in their hands had to be forbidden from washing their hands from 10.00 a.m. to 6:00 p.m. during the very hot weather, otherwise the water would burn their hands.

Outside the hospital gates, numerous beggars gathered every day. One man, lying on a low trolley, manoeuvred himself round, just getting out of the way of cars and people, holding out his hand for money. However, a friend of ours got to the hospital very early one morning and saw this man walking and whistling down the street, carrying his trolley. As soon as he reached the gates, he lay down his trolley and appeared to be a cripple!

In the winter in daytime, it was still hot enough to wear just a short-sleeved shirt. Poor people, who were the majority of the population, did not have electricity in their homes and therefore had no ceiling fans. Nor could they escape to the hills during the very hot summer months, which Western people did. We wondered whether that was the reason why so many of them looked tired and resigned. However, in addition to that, as we learnt about the Hindu religion, we realised that the caste system produced a fatalistic outlook. The Hindu priests or Brahmins were in the top caste, rulers and warriors below them, then merchants and minor officials, then unskilled workers, and at the very bottom religiously and socially Untouchables or Outcasts or Dalits. Dalits do extremely dirty and menial tasks, and the ones who do the foulest (unmentionable) jobs are allowed to come out on the streets only at night. Dalits had extreme difficulty in acquiring an education – often only given by Christian agencies. Even to this day in many areas, a high caste woman will hitch up her sari when she passes an Outcast. Marriage can only be within your caste.

Hindus believe that each of us is involved in an almost-endless cycle of reincarnation. How you behaved in a previous life determines your status in the present life, and that predicts how you will spend all your life. A human might be reincarnated as an animal, and so you cannot kill the monkey that is eating your crops; and no true Hindu will eat meat. This made a lot of the people anaemic, which also contributed to their tiredness. If you developed leprosy, you had certainly been evil in your previous life and were now paying the price.

The Gospel of Jesus Christ teaches that all people are equal; we only have one life, and everyone can receive salvation by repentance towards God. This 'Good News' was especially welcome among Outcasts and leprosy patients.

Among the vast number of very poor village people, girls were considered a burden, as they could only get married with the aid of a dowry, which would leave the family in debt for several years. So these village parents would not be unhappy to receive money for their young daughters, who would then be 'married' to a Hindu god, but in fact had to provide sexual services in the Hindu temples. A hundred years ago, a Christian woman, Amy Carmichael, set about the risky task of rescuing these young girls from the temples and made a home for them in Dohnavur, South India.

There was also a minority Muslim population, and in the villages there would be three areas for the houses of Hindus, Muslims and Christians. If you changed your religion, you had to move house!

I was pregnant with Caroline, whose birth was due the following April. However, in September, because of the heat, I was running a continuous fever – not good when you're pregnant. I had developed an infection, but afterwards my temperature failed to return to normal. We heard that in Palmaner, a village three thousand feet up and an hour's drive away, there was a residential school for Indian village girls run by an American lady. The girls were taught home skills, childcare and embroidery. We were delighted when we heard from her that we could stay there for a week.

The Vellore hospital engineer had a little old car, and he kindly transported us there. With our small salary we could not afford to buy or maintain a car. It was such pleasure to have cool early mornings. The house-boy wore his woolly hat, but he still wore shorts and had bare legs and bare feet! Ruth also enjoyed the change in climate and promptly started to crawl. Stewart was asked to lead Bible studies for the Indian girls. Fortunately, my temperature soon returned to normal, and we returned to the CMC.

Keeping my prenatal appointments with the doctor who was five miles away in the Vellore City Hospital became quite an ordeal. The traffic from CMC to the hospital was horrendous with erratic cars, bicycles, pedicabs, pedestrians, numerous beggars, cows and children who ran across the road to pick up their dung, which they used as fuel. It was no wonder that my doctor found that my blood pressure was raised whenever she took it, much to her concern. However, to our relief, in due course our lovely baby daughter Caroline was born in mid-April with no problems.

After four months in our single room in the Big Bungalow, we were very glad that a two-room unit in a small block nearby became available for us – privacy at last! We moved there in November 1960 and stayed there for two months. Ruth had her first birthday on December 5th, and I wrote about it to Stewart's parents:

> Ruth has been looking such a smart girl today, in the lovely little red romper suit you sent for her. She's been very happy on this her first birthday and is very 'busy' playing. Her hair has grown so much and is quite curly. She has had some illnesses in this heat, but for the most part she is a very happy little girl, and a very dear and precious one.

Ruth did get attacks of diarrhoea; then she had to live on small amounts of heavily boiled, salted rice and plenty of drinks.

At that time, we had the great news that Stewart's old Housemaster from Repton School was coming to visit us in India. He had followed our movements and was now retired. The bonus was that he was able to bring a few things out from England for us. I really wanted a nice maternity dress, which I definitely could not find in Vellore, and some useful baby things. My kind father in England went shopping and found just the right dress for me. He always had very good taste. I was overjoyed, and we had a great time with our friend from England, who much enjoyed travelling to the countryside with leprosy workers and seeing what they did.

When he got back to England he was able to show his slides and told people of the work that he saw. He wrote to Stewart's mother:

> I had a wonderful visit of four days to Stewart and Jean. They were splendid hosts! I greatly enjoyed being with them. Ruth recognised in this ancient grandfather a kindred spirit, and we got on well together. I was really pleased to find them all looking so well, especially Jean and Ruth. Stewart, like everyone else at Vellore, works hard but seems none the worse for it. The society there is certainly inspiring. Stewart gave me a wonderful insight into the work of the hospital and especially his own work among the leprosy patients. I sat in an outpatient clinic, attended an afternoon session for dressings, watched the physiotherapists at work, joined in the ward rounds, and saw the Leprosarium and the Rehabilitation Centre, and the Roadside Clinic at work.

As Christmas approached, we were invited to the 'New Life Village' Christmas Carol Service. This Village had been founded by Paul Brand for young men with leprosy paralysis of their hands or feet, where they could live while they had their operations. They learnt how to do a trade and work in the field and home without damaging their anaesthetic hands. However, not only did they get a new physical life but they were taught about Jesus, and nearly all of them learnt to love Him as their Saviour – New Life indeed! We went there on a beautiful, warm south-Indian winter's evening, with a starry sky overhead. No electricity of course, just one or two pressure lanterns. It was very a moving experience for us to sit in the open air with the patients and listen to them singing their Christmas carols with such feeling. It was an experience that we will never forget.

Then in January 1961 we moved to the large Leprosy Research Sanatorium and Hospital at Karigiri, ten miles outside the city of Vellore. As is common, such a leprosy hospital is never welcome near a town, but four thousand outpatients receive their treatment there. Three hospital wards and seven cottages housed one hundred and fifty patients receiving surgery, long-term physiotherapy and those receiving new anti-leprosy drugs. Staff prayers were held each morning.

In Karigiri, we lived in the separate staff area in a large house with cool verandahs, occupying two bedrooms on the top floor and a dining room and kitchen on the bottom floor. An adjoining room on the ground floor was occupied by a nurse from Burma, who was also studying leprosy work. While she was in India, she heard of Jesus and his salvation for the first time. She decided to trust Him as her Saviour and Lord, much to the anger of two young Burmese doctors, who were also studying leprosy work in Vellore and Karigiri. They were firmly of the opinion that it was unpatriotic for a Buddhist Burmese to become a Christian.

The wife of the Indian Superintendent of the Karigiri Sanatorium lived in a neighbouring bungalow and loved to play Indian music, which would waft over to our bungalow. We were pleased that Silas, one of the other trainee surgeons, came out to see us in Karigiri.

In Karigiri we had a part-time ayah, Julie, and we employed her husband, Nayagam, as our cook. They both spoke English. We needed their local knowledge. For example, because the only source of milk was a person who brought a bucket of buffalo milk to our house, I was taught to put an ordinary hygrometer into the milk to check that it had not been diluted with water. As the bucket or the water might have been very dirty, the milk was boiled before we drank it. We also had a gardener, Ganesar, attached to our house, who grew lovely flowers and was always very concerned about snakes in our area. One day he mimed the hissing of a snake and pointed to the drainpipe coming down from the bathroom. Fortunately there was a wire grating over the top of the drain in the corner of the bathroom. When I poured hot water down the drain, a snake did indeed come out, which Ganesar killed with great relish. He counted it a huge privilege to come and help in the house, as he wanted to learn about housework.

Each evening after our evening meal, we invited Julie and Nayagam to join us while we read a short passage from the Bible. One day Nayagam asked if he could choose the passage. He chose Psalm 34 verse 6: "This poor man called, and the Lord heard him." Then he said, "I am a very poor man!"

The only way we were able to stay at a reasonable temperature without air-conditioning was to shut the windows at dawn and put on all the fans in the house. In the cool of the evenings, I had a daily walk with Ruth in her pushchair to see the mongoose families that lived around the lake. They were enchanting in the way they played around, though I never saw them catch a snake. We also enjoyed watching chameleons changing colour. Once the sun had set in the evening, the darkness descended very quickly without any twilight or dusk, just black night.

While we were in Karigiri my pregnancy was progressing uneventfully. However, on one dark evening when Stewart and I were out for a walk in the cooler air, I suddenly noticed a snake crawling across the path and had to jump high in the air – not easy when you are eight months pregnant.

Stewart performed a lot of operations on leprosy-damaged hands, feet and faces, and learnt how to perfect his technique. There were also daily outpatient clinics and reviews in the Physiotherapy Department. One day, in the outpatient clinic was a most beautiful young Indian woman who, with her devoted husband, had come five hundred miles to Karigiri; but Stewart was shocked at her stumps of hands and the large ulcers on the soles of both feet because she had lost feeling. Sadly, she had come far too late for her hands to be made useful.

The surgical and physiotherapy team from Karigiri used to go into Vellore Leprosy Unit every week by hospital bus for meetings and teaching. A driver was not always available, and as Stewart had obtained his Indian driving licence, once or twice he drove the bus from Karigiri.

On one occasion they were late, and Stewart was driving slightly faster than usual when his colleague Sam leaned over his shoulder and said, "Don't go too fast through this village. A few weeks ago a bus driver went through fast and a small child in the village ran out onto the road and was run over. The villagers stopped the bus and hanged the bus driver from a neighbouring tree!" Stewart drove more slowly after that.

After two months in Karigiri, the Nursing Matron left to go on leave back to New Zealand. We were able to afford to buy her a Vespa scooter, which proved to be invaluable when we went up to the Nilgiri Hills for our holiday.

When our daughter Caroline was born – on April 12th – the nearest midwife was in the Vellore CMC Hospital, and so Stewart had to borrow the Karigiri hospital car and drive me at night to the hospital. In the heat, villagers would lie by the side of the road and even *in* the road; so Stewart had to be rather careful. We finally got to Vellore, and I was rushed up to the delivery suite. Just as our lovely second daughter Caroline was about to be born, a midwife appeared, and Stewart was grateful to retire.

As the year wore on, the heat built up, and by April all the European and American staff had left to stay in the hills for two months until the rains came and the weather became slightly cooler. However, The Leprosy Mission had made no provision for us as a family to go to the hills; presumably they thought that Dr Brand would do something, but he was always much too busy. So we asked around to find names of people who owned houses there, and Stewart wrote to them asking if we could rent one for the holiday. Miraculously, one lady agreed to rent us her bungalow called 'Beracah' (from the Bible book of Chronicles) – apparently because Stewart put a Bible verse at the top of his letter to her. Beracah was located two miles through a forest outside the small city of Kotagiri in the Nilgiri Hills, about five thousand feet above sea level – much cooler than the plain – and overlooking a tea plantation. We arranged for Julie and Nayagam to travel up there two days before we arrived, buy some food and open the house.

Caroline was just ten days old when we caught the overnight train to the Nilgiri Hills. Stewart had failed to bribe the railway booking staff, and so we had to share our train compartment with a large Indian man and Stewart had to sleep on the floor. We took our scooter on the train with us. When we got to the station at the bottom of the mountain, the two girls and I caught the bus up to the top while Stewart followed on his scooter. The bus had to make various stops on the way, to let people on and off. While on the bus, local Indian women were most kind in helping with Ruth, while I held Caroline. The bus could go faster than the small scooter, and I was always relieved to see Stewart passing us while the bus stopped. He waved periodically as we passed each other. When the bus reached Kotagiri, Stewart got a taxi for us and followed on his scooter. We wound through the forest and finally reached Beracah.

At five thousand feet we had a wonderful view each morning of fluffy, white clouds below us hovering over the tea plantations; but as the house was isolated, no-one would come our way unless they came specially to visit. We were remarkably cold our first night and so had to take down the curtains to use as blankets on the bed. Julie and Nayagam had requested extra pay for staying in such a remote and 'dangerous' place. They were petrified of the forest that came up to the back of our house and were convinced that if they ventured out beyond the wall of our small garden then a wild animal would eat them. Not many years before – so the story went – an artist had been painting in the forest about a hundred yards from our bungalow and when he looked up he saw a tiger! He got up and ran for his life.

In fact, one morning, we realised that a lethal creature had come very near us when we woke to find a King Cobra had shed its ten-foot skin on our porch! Apparently, death from the bite of a King Cobra can occur within thirty minutes. We took a photo of the skin but fortunately never saw a live one. King Cobras have a particular liking for tea plantations.

We sent a telegram to Stewart's mother in England saying we would value her help at this time, and we were delighted to hear that she was able to join us in India. When she sent her reply telegram back, the text we received said, "Coming Monday." Stewart found a reliable taxi in Kotagiri that would take him down to Coimbatore Airport at the foot of the mountains to meet his mother on the Monday. Imagine our surprise when on the Sunday evening at 10:00 p.m. our front door bell rang, and there was Stewart's mother complete with hat, umbrella and English newspaper! She had sent her telegram "Coming Sunday" but the Indian telegraph system had somehow changed it to "Monday"!

She was surprised that she was not met at the airport, and we were amazed that she had found her own way up from the airport on a bus to the centre of Kotagiri; and then got a taxi which she persuaded to come out through the forest at night two miles to us. It was lovely to have her, and she enjoyed being with her two first grandchildren.

There was a small Anglican Christian church in the town of Kotagiri, with a kind, elderly English clergyman. He agreed to baptise Caroline, and it was wonderful to have 'Granny' with us for the service. After our enjoyable break in the cool of the hills, she came back to Karigiri and stayed for a few weeks with us. She had been (and remained) on the Council of The Leprosy Mission in England for several years. Stewart's parents had worked in a leprosy hospital in China in 1940, and she was most interested to see the work at Karigiri and also the Vellore Leprosy Unit. However, it was still incredibly hot, and difficult to sleep. Ruth was very restless.

Then, in mid-July in the early hours of the morning, we heard an amazing noise. It was frogs croaking because the rains had come – and what a relief it was for us too. Our local pond in the hospital grounds filled with water, and the frogs now thrived. Presumably they had survived deep under the mud waiting for the rains to come.

Stewart's mother wrote about her time with us:

> *I always went to the 7:30 a.m. service on Sundays, conducted in the Tamil language. All of the congregation left their shoes outside, and most sat on the ground. About twenty small boy patients sat in front very quietly and never disturbed the time of meditation that preceded the service. White walls, white Communion Table, white clothes of most of those present, and two tall candlesticks on the ground with fluttering flame. Rhythmical Indian lyrics were sung unaccompanied. One of the Indian staff read from the Bible, and another staff member gave the talk. We felt that God in His love was truly with us; and not one, not even the many Hindu patients, could fail to perceive it.*

After our year in India, we were due to leave – on July 27th – to go on to our major work for The Leprosy Mission on an island in Hong Kong waters. We planned to fly to Hong Kong from Madras (now Chennai) on the east coast of India, eighty miles from Vellore, with an overnight stop in Ceylon. Our trunks with our crockery, cutlery, books and clothes, and the pram in a crate, were taken ahead of our departure by the Karigiri Hospital van to Madras. A few days before we left, Stewart had to go by bus to Madras to check that the trunks and crate had indeed reached the port and were ready to be loaded.

Leaving from our remote leprosy hospital in Karigiri was an event in itself. We had to make all our own arrangements, and Stewart found what he thought was a reliable taxi and driver to take us to Madras airport. On the morning of the flight, we loaded up the car with our two girls, our possessions and ourselves, and set off. The driver seemed to drive in a surprisingly cautious way and was not keen to go fast. When asked, he said that one of his tyres was very worn, and he was keen to preserve it. But we did have a plane to catch. So we stopped the taxi halfway to Madras, primarily to allow me to feed Caroline, who was now four months old. Stewart decided that he would have to drive if we were to get to the airport in time, but the car refused to re-start! As we were wondering how to start the taxi, very fortunately a large bus containing students hove in sight. Stewart stood in the middle of the road and flagged it to a stop. The students willingly got out and gave us a push-start, and the engine fired up. Stewart drove somewhat faster, much to the consternation of the Indian driver, but we reached the airport just in time for our flight.

This was the first aeroplane flight either of us had undertaken, but the stewardesses on the flight were very helpful and kind. We stayed overnight in Ceylon, and in our hotel Ruth enjoyed the experience of a bath for the first time since England. Only showers had been available in India. The next day we flew into Hong Kong, and a glorious sunrise greeted us.

CHAPTER FOUR

Three years on a leprosy island off Hong Kong

$\mathcal{A}$s our plane flew into Hong Kong, we saw numerous small islands around the main island of Hong Kong. The azure ocean sparkled, and many Chinese 'junks'[9] were sailing on the sea. We flew low over the harbour, before touching down on the airport runway that jutted out from the peninsula of Kowloon – the nearest end of the 'New Territories' which extended back twenty-two miles to the border with China.

Hong Kong had many familiar sights, sounds and smells, which were evocative of the many months I had spent there in 1945. It is one of my favourite places, and for me it felt like coming home. I have seen it change over the years from immediately post-war in 1945, when it was struggling to recover from the Japanese occupation, to our final visit in 1996 during one of Stewart's medical conferences. By then, skyscrapers and modern hotels had taken over from the Chinese street markets, and the 'Old China' shops seemed to have vanished. But the spectacular waterfront, lit up at night and reflected in the harbour, was always (and remains) a wonderful sight.

During our three years in Hong Kong from 1961 it was under British rule. At that time, we heard of the terrible purges and dragooning of the populace into communes that was occurring in Communist China. There had been a great famine in the previous three years, when at least forty million people died. This was due to Mao's policy of exporting food to other Communist countries while harvests in China were very poor, but he insisted they were good.

---

[9] boats

When Mao's Deputy Ruler of the country, Liu Shao-chi, visited his sister in the countryside, he found her dying, and her husband had already died of starvation.

When we arrived in Hong Kong, a cholera epidemic was raging, but only ten people died due to the excellent medical facilities. So we had to be careful eating salad and any other uncooked food.

At Hong Kong airport, we were met by a few of the expatriate (non-Chinese) staff of The Leprosy Mission, who were working on the leprosy island known in Chinese as 'Hay Ling Chau' – Isle of Happy Healing. After our arrival, we had lunch at the YMCA building (Young Men's Christian Association). Ruth was not used to having so many people interested in her and was rather bemused by everything.

Hay Ling Chau (HLC) was one hour by boat from Hong Kong island, out in the South China Sea. With our two little daughters and our luggage, we boarded the HLC launch – the 'Ling Hong'. Memories came flooding back. The harbour was alive with small craft of all descriptions – not only the traditional junks but also sophisticated Western motor launches and the Star Ferry that constantly sailed between Hong Kong island and Kowloon. These ferries were always crowded, and the boat listed alarmingly on its arrival at the pier with the crowds of people rushing to get off. There is a mountain on the top of Hong Kong island called The Peak, and it was possible to see the railway that climbed up almost vertically from the harbour to the top of the Peak.

HLC had no resident population until 1951, when it was designated as the site for the hospital for more severely affected leprosy patients. Approaching the HLC quayside, the red flowering flame trees stood out – a splendid sight. We were pleased to meet many of the Chinese staff who had come to greet us. Three Chinese doctors and most of the nurses arrived on the Ling Hong on Monday mornings and left on Friday evenings to join their families in Hong Kong. The five hundred resident patients lived in small cottages in the main valley of the island, away from the residences of the staff. When we arrived, the other expatriates on the island were four single people – Grace, an Australian woman surgeon; Joyce, a nurse; Jean, the physiotherapist; an older man, Jim, The Leprosy Mission Secretary for the Far East, and the English administrator, Alan, who was married with two small girls.

We were settled at first in the Guest Bungalow. It was near the area where the Chinese staff had their residences, with a steep road down to the jetty, and about halfway to the hospital. There, we were looked after by two Chinese amahs who cleaned and cooked – they loved Ruth and baby Caroline. Unfortunately, our luggage coming from India had not been put on the ship booked for it and did not arrive in Hong Kong until two months after we arrived.

So it was not until the beginning of October that we were able to move into a bungalow of our own, in an area of the island out of bounds for the patients, over a hill on the other side of the main jetty bay. At the end of our small garden a large cliff dropped steeply down into the sea. A sturdy fence had been built to protect our children. I wrote in a letter:

> It is the first time since we were married two and a half years ago that we have a house to ourselves with all our belongings! We revel in the superb views over the sea to the large island of Lantau, and then on to the islands outside the British territorial waters, which are part of Communist China. The extreme nearness of our huge, hungry neighbour is perhaps not obvious to tourists who see only Hong Kong's many skyscrapers. One intelligent Chinese man told Stewart the other day, "I hear of what is going on in China and I am afraid."

We had three bedrooms and so were able to have a resident Chinese girl as our own amah. She was called Ah Fong and had been working as a lift-girl in a Hong Kong block of flats. When she was young, she had escaped across the border into Hong Kong with her father; but her mother was still in Communist China, whom she had not seen for many years. In those days, Communist China banned virtually everyone from travelling in and out of Hong Kong. Leprosy patients were the exception! As they could come freely into Hong Kong, quite a leprosy problem had developed in the Colony.

Ah Fong was really pleased to come and see us on HLC, but she spoke very little English. I asked the two amahs who worked at the Guest Bungalow to explain to her what her work would involve and the implications of living on a leprosy island. I liked Ah Fong and trained her in our Western ways and how to look after our girls. I wrote in a letter:

> *We have given Ah Fong a New Testament, and we read the Bible with her quite often.*

To save money on the island, electricity to the staff houses was limited to the time between 4:00 p.m. and midnight. This was certainly arranged for the staff who worked in the hospital during the daytime but ignored the needs of the two households with children and a mother at home. We had a pedestal fan that we could move around our house, but it would have been nice to have had a fan in the heat of the day, including when I was cooking in the kitchen! We had no air-conditioning, or electric washing-machine or dishwasher, and no disposable nappies. All our clothes and dishes had to be washed by hand. In the hot, humid climate and with two very young children, there was a lot of washing to be done! Our stove ran on gas from a cylinder and our refrigerator on kerosene. Sadly, Ruth still woke for two or three hours every night, as she had done since we arrived in India. It was not until April 1962 that I could write in a letter:

> *We are rejoicing in answered prayer that Ruth is much more settled, and we have had mostly unbroken nights recently.*

In Hong Kong and Kowloon, simple shops still abounded, but with our young children I was not able to get there often. There were compensations for us, as we understood Chinese people and we loved the beauty of the ever-changing sea.

The Ling Hong boat was berthed each evening back in Hong Kong, and every morning, except on Sunday, it brought our food and visitors to the island. On HLC there were no shops and no telephone contact with the main island of Hong Kong, except in an emergency from a small Marine Police post on a corner of the island near us. The only way that I could order food or household items for our family was from

71

a Chinese man called Ah Kwan, who would take my order in the Cantonese dialect of Chinese every day. He then purchased all the items and the next day brought them. Ah Kwan had a marvellous memory and would remember all I asked him to purchase. However, he spoke very little English. So it was a steep learning curve for me to master all the Cantonese words for the food, vegetables and household items that I had to order from Ah Kwan every day!

Stewart and I started Cantonese language lessons, not only to speak to Ah Fong, Ah Kwan and other Chinese helpers in the houses, but Stewart had to communicate with the patients, very few of whom spoke English. He continued with Cantonese lessons every morning for the first six months. I persevered with my lessons for a while, but in due course I learnt more from Ah Fong. I also listened and learnt on the inter-island ferry to and from Hong Kong, which we occasionally took.

As youngsters, Stewart and I had lived in a Mandarin-speaking area of China, and we rapidly found that these two main languages of China are very different. Cantonese has been described as one of the hardest languages in the world to learn. All words are made up of one-syllable sounds, but each syllable (in Hong Kong) has to be spoken in one of six tones, and each tone has a different meaning. For example, the word 'ee' for the top tone means 'healing', and other tones mean 'ear', 'two', and 'now'! The word 'say' can mean 'four' or 'death'. Chinese superstition was so prevalent that the Chinese were unhappy with four in their house, car and telephone numbers. We also had to learn how the Chinese language is more sophisticated than English. For example, there are three words for 'thank you' – one for a task done, one for a gift, and another for a sympathetic word.

The initial plan had been that there would be a physician on HLC and Stewart would be the surgeon. However, just before we had gone to India for Stewart to learn leprosy surgery, the HLC physician had been invalided home to England. Grace had been brought in at short notice, and she loved doing surgery. She insisted that she did all the hand and foot operations. However, she had not been trained in plastic surgery, and there were some cured patients who had to stay on the island because they had sunken noses due to leprosy and would never be accepted back into Chinese society. In due course,

Stewart was able to 'remake' several noses, and the patients happily returned to their homes in Hong Kong.

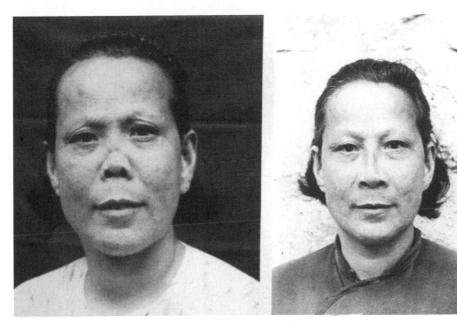

Leprosy nose remade

Stewart learnt the hospital routine, and as he had studied eye diseases in England he made a thorough examination of the eyes of all the patients, because leprosy can invade the eye. Another eye disease, trachoma, is extremely common in China, and he checked all the patients for it and was able to treat many of them before it caused much damage. In fact, in 1964 when our small family returned to England, we were all found to have early trachoma and needed appropriate treatment.

In early 1962, Stewart was very excited to discover that he could detect early leprosy paralysis and reverse it! A sign of leprosy, even in patients with normal-looking hands, is that when the nerves near the skin in the arm and leg are pressed, the patient experiences pain (the nerve is tender). It occurred to Stewart that this pain could indicate that there was already some damage in the nerve. So in these patients he decided to test the strength of each muscle in the hand and leg. On my old manual typewriter (no computers in those days) I typed out the name of each of these muscles for a chart, and Stewart then graded the strength of each muscle. He was electrified to find that in

73

these patients with normal finger movement but tender nerves, the strength of many of the muscles was already considerably weakened!

One day, while he was testing the hands and feet of such patients, the physiotherapist Jean passed by. She asked, "What are you doing?"

Stewart replied, "I am testing the strength of each muscle and grading them from 0 to 4 (full strength)."

She then said, "There is already an international method of grading muscle strength called the 'Voluntary Muscle Test' (VMT) with a grading from 0 to 5."

Stewart explained that he was finding that many of these patients had very weak muscles, and he asked if she and her staff would have time to help do these tests, to which she kindly agreed. Then Stewart devised appropriate drug treatment and rest of the limb, and was thrilled to find that nearly all these weak muscles recovered their strength, helped by exercises that he and the physiotherapist devised.

Thus he was probably the first doctor in the world to detect and reverse early leprosy nerve damage. He prevented his patients getting paralysed and also, importantly, they did not lose the feeling in their hands. However, his description of this in a medical article was delayed for several years by our isolation on HLC and his inexperience in writing such articles. When we were in Ethiopia later, Stewart found that also in African patients early detection of nerve damage and its reversal was possible in nearly all his patients. It was not until 1976 that the International Leprosy Congress first discussed this problem and the solution! The Congress was held in Mexico City, and Stewart was asked to be the first speaker.

For patients in whom their leprosy had caused a sunken nose, Stewart used a skin graft inside the nose and a bone graft for the bridge of the nose. The patients quite liked their 'European' appearance! One man had lost his nose entirely, and his eyebrows. Stewart created a new nose for him from his skin of his forehead and transplanted hair for his eyebrows. He then happily left the island. Leprosy can cause swelling of the skin of the face, so that after treatment the skin is like that of an old person. Stewart did face-lifts on these patients and made them look young again.

Our whole purpose in volunteering to work for The Leprosy Mission was to bring the love and message of Jesus to leprosy patients by word and deed. So we were delighted to support Pastor Eugene Gia, who was not a leprosy patient and was the Chinese pastor on Hay Ling Chau. He had been a Lutheran pastor in Hong Kong but learnt of the need of a pastor on HLC. Having been brought up as a Mandarin Chinese speaker, he had to acquire Cantonese while he lived in Hong Kong as a refugee from the mainland of China. He bravely decided to come and work among the leprosy patients and the fifty Chinese staff on our island, and had a great love for all the patients. He was among the most energetic Chinese we have ever met and always had a twinkle in his eye, building up a fine congregation of Christians among the leprosy patients and ministering to the Chinese staff during the week.

The church building on the island was called 'The Lord is Willing Church' (in Cantonese) after the verse in Mark's Gospel chapter 1, in which Jesus was approached by a leprosy patient who said, "If you are willing, you can make me clean." Jesus touched the patient and said, "I am willing. Be clean!" and immediately the leprosy left him. Thus the church was appropriately named after the fact that Jesus was, and is, "willing". Stewart was able to attend the church services more frequently than I could. There were particularly wonderful services at Christmas and Easter. I was able to get to the church for a Communion service for the first time on October 1st and was welcomed by Pastor Gia.

Although the staff bungalow area was out of bounds for the patients, we were happy that on our first Christmas Eve at 11:00 p.m. the patients' choir, together with Pastor Gia, came and sang carols outside our house. We gave them each a small stocking with sweets. I had been round the wards with Stewart for carol singing.

Just after Christmas I wrote in a letter:

> We are certainly getting very attached to the patients. They are always so grateful and cheerful – and brave. We have had many of the Chinese staff in for tea or coffee. Our children were given so many presents, we were almost overwhelmed. We had all the expatriate staff in for New Year's Day tea – it was a happy time.

Stewart's diary recorded how we regularly invited our Western colleagues in for meals, but unfortunately it turned out that it was not easy to form real friendships.

On our first Easter Saturday, I wrote:

I was able to go with Stewart to Communion on Maundy Thursday[10] evening. There is something about taking Communion with a choir of leprosy patients singing behind one, and giving one's empty cup into the crippled hands of an ex-patient. There will be eight baptisms after church on Easter morning.

The patients who were brought to HLC were the ones who had more severe leprosy or leprosy deformities. So it is not surprising that during our first eighteen months three patients committed suicide and two were rescued from suicide. Virtually every patient who came to our island was a Buddhist. In Buddhism, any tragedy in this life, including leprosy, is the result of a bad deed done in your previous life (your Karma). As leprosy is such a terrible disease, for a woman this usually was ascribed to immorality in her previous life. How depressed she would feel! It came as wonderful news to all our patients, many of whom had disfigured faces and hands, that Jesus taught that we all have only one life. If we confess our sins, He will forgive us our sins and give us salvation and peace; and all who believe in Him will live with Him in the next life, with a wonderful body "as the angels in heaven" [11]. About a fifth of the patients accepted Jesus as their Saviour and Lord and regularly worshipped in The Lord is Willing Church.

On one or two occasions we were driven by friends in Hong Kong to look at different Buddhist temples. On the steps of these temples, it was sad to see distraught Chinese women banging their heads and lighting their incense sticks. Each would also have a container with marked 'sticks', and shake and empty this repeatedly, looking for signs of 'good luck'. With the statues and incense inside the temple, I felt an evil influence emanating from them, and I could not go inside, as many tourists like to do.

Most Chinese are imprisoned in a web of superstition. For any occasion such as a wedding, funeral or shop-opening, an astrologer will be consulted and an auspicious day and hour chosen. Each year and each day of the Chinese lunar month has its portent for good or evil. What is done on the tenth day ('the big day') will be either very good or very bad. Washing your hair is bad!

---

[10] the day before Good Friday
[11] Mark 12:25

Two beaches on the island were reserved for staff. It was lovely to have access to them, and the nearest was only about ten minutes' walk from our bungalow down a steep path to the sand. Many an afternoon, I would take Ruth and Caroline down for an afternoon's swim. They loved putting their swimming rings on and paddling out into the bay. Two years later, after Timothy was born and he was at the crawling stage, he would determinedly follow his sisters on hands and knees towards the water. I frequently had to rescue him before his head went under the waves! Occasionally, a large pleasure launch would aim for our beach. However, when they got to us we would say, "Do you know this is a leprosy island?" They always immediately turned round and sailed quickly away!

I have always collected shells in whichever seaside place I have found myself around the world, starting when I was a child in Chefoo. Our beaches on HLC were a treasure trove for me. Since then I have collected shells on the west coast of Ireland and shells of all sizes when we later lived in other countries – and also in many holiday places including the Seychelles, which we visited in the years to come while I was travelling with Stewart on his medical conferences and lecture tours. I have acquired a big collection.

As there was no air-conditioning on the island, except in the hospital operating room, we found sleeping a problem in the hot summer months – from April to October – as it was also extremely humid. Even in May, the temperature could reach 36°C (94°F). We had electricity from 4:00 p.m. But at midnight, when the electricity went off, we would all wake up drenched in perspiration. In due course, we discovered that a helpful solution was to put a thin bamboo mat under the bottom sheet and a small thin mat under the pillowcase, on top of the pillow. This made an enormous difference, allowing more circulation of air, and allowed us to sleep.

We encountered many difficulties living in the heat, humidity and isolation on the island, in a very small community, but one of our pleasures was enjoying the company of our two beautiful little daughters. In April 1962 I wrote:

> *Ruth has unbounded faith in her Daddy's abilities 'to make people better', and one of her favourite occupations is making her dollies better. Sometimes she is busy doing language study, or pretending to be our language teacher.*

And later:

> *Ruth is becoming increasingly fond of books as she understands more. Caroline is developing a lot just now. She won't eat unless she's 'helping'! She waves bye-bye to Stewart when he goes off to the hospital, and says 'Amen' very emphatically after grace[12]. She and Ruth laugh at each other just for the fun of it. It's priceless to see them. Caroline's hair is quite curly – more so than Ruth's was. Ruth has thick hair which grows so fast. She talks more and more, and in Cantonese. I have a job to keep pace with her!*

About a mile away from HLC was an island called Peng Chau, which was a stopping point for the ferries from Hong Kong to the outer islands. We could be taken there by a small HLC motor launch called the 'Hay Ling' that was berthed on our island, and then we could catch a ferry into Hong Kong. Later in the day, we came back on another ferry and could arrange to be picked up by the Hay Ling from Peng Chau. As the Ling Hong only came out in the morning from Hong Kong and went back in the afternoon, we could not use it for a day trip into Hong Kong. Going via Peng Chau was the only way we could go in, just for the day. However, when Caroline was very young, it was difficult to take her and Ruth into Hong Kong only for a day. I didn't actually visit Hong Kong City until the end of September, two months after we arrived. It was 35°C (94°F) and very humid that day. Up to then, and later, clothes for the children and personal items were bought by Stewart on occasional trips into Hong Kong.

The Ling Hong boat brought visitors who wanted to see the work on our island; but as the boat did not return until 2:00 p.m., a recurring problem was that many visitors had to be given lunch. Those of us who lived on the island used to have to stretch our provisions to cater for extra people, and this happened quite often. We did enjoy meeting new people and made some friends. Later, we were able occasionally to stay overnight away from the island with friends that we made whom we had entertained for lunch. We became good friends with the Vicar of St Andrew's Anglican Church in Kowloon and his wife. They had two children, one the same age as Ruth. It was always a pleasure to stay with them and an opportunity

---

[12] a prayer of thanks to Jesus before each meal

to go to an Anglican church. On other occasions, Stewart would be asked to speak at meetings in Hong Kong, and we would try and go as a family and stay overnight.

About four months after we arrived, we were delighted that my parents were able to come and stay on HLC for a few months. They were with us for our first Christmas on the island, and it was a happy time for us all. They gave us a present of an awning over the sandpit by our house, in which our children played. This was marvellous protection from the sun and meant that the children could play longer out of doors. With my parents' China background and knowledge of post-war Hong Kong, it was interesting for them, and they came to understand the problems of the leprosy patients. My dad was asked on one or two occasions to 'preach' at our 5:00 p.m. Sunday service in the Guest Bungalow for the expatriate staff. He told us about his early days in China, emphasising the power of prayer and how it united the missionaries, and the help from Bible studies together, which we did not have on HLC. My parents were saddened at the lack of unity among the expatriate staff on HLC. (The 5:00 p.m. service was not geared for small children and so I could not go regularly.)

Stewart and I have always devoted a time every day to personal Bible Study and prayer together, and that has been (and still is) our main spiritual 'food'. Of course there are many times during the day when we utter frequent short prayers as needs come, and before our meals. There was, and is, always so much to pray about: for the health and safety of us and our children, and strength to follow the teachings of Jesus and help others.

Unfortunately, not long before my parents were due to leave, my father experienced a sudden 'dissection of the aorta'[13]. It was agonisingly painful. He was very ill and lucky to be alive. We had some very anxious days before he could be transferred to a hospital in Hong Kong. I sent a telegram to my elder brother in England, and he arranged for my other brother Jim to fly out to Hong Kong. Jim stayed for a short time, making arrangements for my parents to fly back with him to London. In England, my father had an excellent family doctor, who cared for him at my sister's house in Purley. He

---

[13] splitting of the wall of the main artery from the heart

required a major heart operation, which fortunately was successful. He did recover but never quite regained his vigour – understandably.

In December 1962, we moved into a new bungalow that had been planned for us. It had three bedrooms for us, a room for Ah Fong and a wide verandah enclosed in wire netting to keep out the mosquitoes. In due course, when patients were more easily cured, we had a cured patient as our gardener for our small garden. He had stayed on the island while Stewart gave him a new nose. Unfortunately, after the operation he got into an argument with a man who hit him on the nose, but thankfully it remained intact! From the new bungalow we again had a clear view of the Lantau, and we could hear the fishermen in their small 'junks' at night. These boats made a distinctive noise, as their engines had a putt-putt sound, and we would hear them going past in the evenings to fish.

The sea was always changing colour: blue, green, azure and deeper hues. However, when the very severe storms came – typhoons[14] – we could be cut off for many days on our island. In the autumn months, particularly, Hong Kong was in the path of tropical storms and typhoons that came sweeping through. I kept a 'typhoon cupboard' ready for such eventualities, with all the necessary provisions, so that we would not starve when a typhoon came. One very severe typhoon called 'Typhoon Wanda' cut us off from the mainland for five days. The mountainous waves prevented the Ling Hong from coming to HLC, and the winds stripped the trees – even the pine trees – of all their leaves and pine needles. The 'eye' of the storm came directly over our island, with the result that between the two directions that occur in a typhoon, there was a period of calm when the wind changed direction and then blew fiercely the other way. During that calm, Stewart rushed off to the hospital to check that patients and staff were alright, and fortunately they were.

The doctor who founded the leprosy work on the island in 1951 was very aware of typhoons. He made sure that every building on HLC had a reinforced concrete roof under the tiles. So there were no injuries from falling debris. Of course, during the fierce wind it was impossible to venture out in safety, and the rain was continuous. We had the radio on all the time, and the news of the shanty towns being

---

[14] hurricanes

washed away from Hong Kong's steep hillsides was dreadful. I wrote in a letter:

> *27 were killed and 27,000 made homeless – tragic. There were gusts of 140 knots, with the wind at 80 knots for 10 hours.*

We always knew when stormy weather was coming, as the fisherfolk headed for the typhoon harbour in their dozens and streamed past our island on their way. Even if the radio announced a typhoon was coming, if the fishermen did not come back past our island we knew that the typhoon would not come our way.

There were several other islands around the main island of Hong Kong, and it was fun to visit these by boat, which we could do occasionally. Lantau Island had several small mountains. At the time we were there, it was entirely rural, including a farm with cows and a Buddhist monastery on one summit. When we went walking there, everyone greeted us warmly. The main mountain on the island was often covered in cloud in the summer, and near the summit was a group of guest houses, where it was possible to stay. In the summer of 1962, we went to Lantau for a week of our holiday to get out of the heat, but with the summit area usually shrouded in mist, we found it somewhat cold for us. Caroline was a small baby at the time, and to get her to sleep Stewart went for long walks carrying her on his back in a Chinese 'sling'.

When we arrived on the island, we were surprised to find that there were no services in the wards, only in the church. This seemed very strange for a Christian hospital. There were staff prayers every morning in the hospital in Cantonese, and Stewart was pleased when he was able to take them, and read from the Chinese Bible. At the end of 1962, Grace left HLC to go for eighteen months' study leave in Sydney, to study for the Fellowship of the Royal Australian College of Surgeons, but without appointing Stewart as her replacement. However, the HK Leprosy Mission Auxiliary, composed of local businessmen, promptly insisted that Stewart was made Acting Medical Superintendent.

One of the first actions Stewart took was to invite Pastor Gia to conduct daily Ward Services in each ward. Space does not allow us to tell of all the wonderful times we had with the patients who had come to our island, sad, ill, and often rejected by their families. We will mention only one of the many who were transformed as a result of hearing about Jesus and believing in Him.

Mr Wong was a father when he developed the most severe form of leprosy. His family was horrified at the potential social problems. His daughters knew that they would never get married if it became known that their father had leprosy. So they confined him to a back room in the house, and as he received no treatment the disease progressed relentlessly. He became blind, his nose collapsed due to damage by leprosy, and the nerves to his hands were destroyed by leprosy bacteria. He lost all feeling in his hands and severely damaged his fingers, and they became just stumps. At this stage his family brought him to the local leprosy clinic, and he was immediately transferred to HLC. He was totally dejected when Stewart admitted him to the ward. We could use anti-leprosy drugs to kill the leprosy bacteria in his body, and our devoted Christian Chinese nurses would dress his ulcers. However, we could not reverse his blindness nor his disfigured face and deformed hands. His family never came to visit him.

People who become blind for causes other than leprosy nearly always retain feeling in their fingers, and this allows them to learn Braille and feel their food and understand their surroundings by touch; but Mr Wong had no sensation in his fingers. So he had no idea where his food was or what it was composed of. He could not avoid walking into a door or a hole, because when he held a stick he could not feel the touch of the stick on a blockage. He was in total isolation except for his hearing. He could never tell if water was hot or cold till it reached his face or body. By the time Mr Wong arrived on our island, Pastor Gia had started Ward Services.

After Mr Wong had been in the ward about three months, one morning when Stewart came into the ward, Mr Wong was smiling! He was still blind and terribly disfigured, and his family had not visited him. This prompted Stewart to ask him (in Cantonese), "Why are you so happy this morning, Mr Wong?"

He replied, "I can feel Jesus in my heart. I know He is my Saviour, and He gives me peace and joy."

He is just one example of the wonderful fact that Jesus and the Holy Spirit are a reality and can come into anyone's heart, soul and mind, and transform their spirit, when they yield to Him. We look forward to meeting Mr Wong in Heaven where he will have a new and perfect body.

Mr Wong stayed on the leprosy island for many years, and in due course he was able to leave the ward and live among fellow patients, who cared for him as he was still blind and deformed. In 1973, we were able to visit HLC again after Stewart had lectured in Australia, and I was with him. Stewart hugged Mr Wong and asked him how he was. He replied, "I have been so happy in Jesus since you left!" In 1985, Stewart again visited Hong Kong, during a medical conference. He took the opportunity to visit Pastor Gia in his retirement home in the New Territories and learnt that Mr Wong's daughter had become a Christian, then trained as a Christian minister and had emigrated to the USA. She had then asked her father to come and live with her. We were so happy for Mr Wong.

While Stewart was the only Western doctor working on the island, he realised that he could make much better use of his time if he had a motor scooter to go down to the jetty to meet visitors and get around the island. He saw a second-hand scooter advertised in Kowloon, just within our meagre means to purchase. With some trepidation he went across and bought it but had to drive down the main road of Kowloon in heavy traffic to get to the launch and to get it back to HLC! It was not only useful for him; when I sat on the pillion seat, Ruth could stand in front of Stewart, and I could cradle Caroline in my arms. So we could go for trips as a family to the more remote and uninhabited part of the island. On one occasion, Stewart took Ruth and Caroline, and they then walked up the highest hill on the island. As the girls sat on a large rock, Stewart was horrified to see a one-foot long, poisonous centipede crawl out from under the rock and then fortunately crawl away!

In 1963, Stewart wrote a small book called 'Essentials of Leprosy for the Clinician'. In it, he gave basic information on how to diagnose and treat leprosy, and included his important discovery of how to detect and treat early leprosy paralysis. There were photographs of a young man whose face had been covered with leprosy patches that disappeared after treatment and a woman whose face had been transformed by one of his nose operations. His book was published by the Hong Kong Auxiliary and all profits went to The Leprosy Mission. The book was bought by visiting doctors and given to the medical students who came to HLC , but after we left Hong Kong it was not re-printed. The Auxiliary actively supported him as he developed a poster campaign throughout the whole colony, which informed the public that a person cured of leprosy should be welcomed back into society.

Stewart did tendon grafts on hands and feet, and devised new operations on the hand to eliminate some of the physical signs of leprosy that many Chinese could recognise, such as the 'sunken' thumb web due to the wasting of paralysed muscles. He inserted plastic-foam into the thumb web. After extensive laboratory work, he made the important discovery that leprosy is primarily spread by live bacteria from the nose, and this became the basis of his Doctor of Medicine thesis for Cambridge University. About the same time, a doctor in India looked at 'nose-blows' and found many bacteria, but he did not correlate this with other laboratory work.

When one new patient arrived with a swollen leg, Stewart recognised that this was due to a parasite in the blood spread by mosquitoes, which can only be detected by a specimen taken during the night. He tested all the patients and staff at night, and found that twenty-four were already infected, but he treated all of them to eliminate the parasite. This meant that mosquitoes on the island could no longer spread the disease.

Our amah, Ah Fong, had a cousin Ah Kwai, who lived in mainland China near the border with Hong Kong. She dreamed of crossing the border into Hong Kong and freedom, but the border was totally closed by guards and the police on both sides did their utmost to deter illegal immigrants crossing into Hong Kong. On a very rainy day, Ah Kwai managed to creep over the border undetected. She contacted her relatives in Hong Kong, and they came and picked her up. Then Ah Fong brought her over to us on the leprosy island. She was convinced that nobody would start looking for her on a leprosy island – true enough! She was a pleasant and lovely, hard-working country girl, and she stayed with us till we left in July 1964. She was a great help, particularly after I had our third child, Timothy, in April 1963.

I became quite attached to Ah Fong, but one morning I woke having had a dreadful dream that she had taken her own life. It disturbed me greatly. An hour later, our island phone rang. When I answered it, I was told that Ah Fong had jumped off the ferry taking her home for the weekend; she was now in hospital. Fortunately, she had been pulled from the water before she drowned. A week later she came back to us, very subdued. I wish I could have done more to help and encourage her. Towards the end of 1963, she chose to go back to Hong Kong. Socially, it had been very lonely for her on the island.

One of Ah Kwai's little Communist habits was to kill flies but then lay them out for me to count! That was what she had to do in Communist China. However, I soon asked her not to do that, and I taught her our Western ways. We also read the Bible with her, and at Christmas she heard the story of the birth of Jesus for the first time in her life. After we left, I was glad that she was able to continue working in one of the other staff houses on HLC.

When we went into Hong Kong we loved shopping at the street markets, which in those days had wonderful, cheap clothes especially for children. Life in Hong Kong was very different from our quiet island, with the bustle, banter and bartering adding to the enjoyment, as we had become fluent in Cantonese. One street was called Cat Street, which had steep steps going uphill. It was a well known place for traditional Chinese shops. We noticed that there were three prices for all items on sale. One price was for the tourists off the cruise ships (the most expensive); a second, cheap price was for local Chinese; and then there was a price midway between these two for foreigners like us who spoke basic Cantonese. Occasionally, I would take Ruth into Hong Kong with me, but she found the streets too busy. A plaintive voice piped up one day, "Mummy, I can't walk; there are too many people," and she was right. It was quite different from the deserted beaches and roads around our house on HLC. But going into Hong Kong was always an experience, and the cheapness of the goods suited our pockets! Thanks to Stewart later attending medical conferences, we have been able to return to Hong Kong at ten year intervals since 1964 and have seen the changes that have taken place. Some are obviously good for the economy, but we miss the old Hong Kong and Kowloon we knew.

While on HLC, one of our favourite places to visit was out in the New Territories, near the town of Shatin. This was an institute set up pre-war by Buddhists who had become Christians, and the buildings and residents were entirely Chinese. It was called 'Dao Fung Saan' –

the Hill of the Holy Spirit – or literally 'Way, Wind Mountain'. Among some hills with lush greenery, the buildings had been built in the old Chinese style with characteristic curved roofs. The residents had a small industry, painting china tiles and plates in the old China style with scenes from the Bible. The Chinese characters beside the pictures were verses from the Bible, and other tiles were painted with Chinese characters such as 'Blessing', 'Peace' and 'Love'. On an adjacent hill was a huge concrete cross with two Chinese characters carved into it, meaning "It is accomplished" – the words that Jesus said on the Cross as He died.

In the side of the hill was a small chapel, and I remembered visiting it when I was in Hong Kong in 1945. A low entrance made people stoop as they went in, and the Chinese words carved over the door were "Lay down your burden." From inside the chapel as you came out, over the door were written the words "Take up your cross." It was a very special place. There was a guesthouse nearby, where visitors could stay for two or three nights, and we stayed there twice during our time in Hong Kong.

When Stewart had opened the Vacation Bible School for the child patients on HLC, speaking in Cantonese he asked if any child had heard of the Lord Jesus before coming to HLC, and not one of the forty children had! When Ruth heard that many boys and girls in Hong Kong did not know of the Lord Jesus, she said, "Well, we had better go and tell them then, hadn't we?!"

During 1962, I became pregnant with Timothy and had my pre-natal check-ups with a nice lady doctor. She worked at the Queen Mary Hospital in the city of Victoria, on the main island of Hong Kong. Timothy was due to be born in April 1963. Stewart had a cousin Mary who was also Caroline's godmother – a trained nurse and midwife, with a brother and his family in New Zealand, whom she regularly visited. On her way home from a visit to New Zealand she stayed with us for a month before and after Timothy was born, and she was a great help. We found it a real godsend at this time, and we were able to do some interesting trips with her before the birth. One trip was to the small Portuguese colony of Macau (founded in 1557), across the other side of the wide Pearl River delta. We set off with Ruth and Caroline, and caught the boat to Hong Kong, and then the hovercraft from Hong Kong to Macau. The hovercraft went at great speed, and this was our first experience of such fast craft. We much enjoyed our weekend on Macau, exploring the different types of architecture, including a Portuguese cathedral built three hundred years earlier. Macau is a small city but has many large casinos and many brothels. It was a very different atmosphere to what we were used to.

It was not long before Timothy decided it was time to arrive. The question was: how would I reach the hospital in Hong Kong if it was in the middle of the night, with no ferries running from any of the neighbouring islands? Fortunately, the Police Post on our island was very cooperative, and when I went into labour they sent a message to the Hong Kong hospital that I was coming. At the start of my labour pains, Stewart took me on his motor scooter down to the jetty, where a police launch was waiting for me. On our way to the jetty, Stewart had to pause when I had strong contractions! Joyce, the nurse, also came on the police launch, which was a very fast, powerful boat that skimmed over the waves giving a smooth ride. However, the journey in the ambulance from the Hong Kong jetty to the hospital went round a lot of hairpin bends and was much bumpier.

Timothy was born on the afternoon of April 25th, the day after I arrived at the hospital. In May I wrote:

> *Timothy is fine and growing well. He has decided ideas of his own and is a strong baby. His hair is getting fairer each day, almost coppery sometimes. Caroline just loves him and plays with his toes 'This little pig went to market...' She likes to brush his hair and give him hugs.*

During the first half of 1963, Hong Kong experienced the start of a severe drought. After Timothy was born and we returned to HLC, one of the first things I did was to ask Stewart to take me on his scooter to the small reservoir on our island which provided all our water. I was horrified to see that our reservoir had become a muddy puddle with green algae, and a dead fish floating in it; and I had to bath my baby boy in this water! I immediately picked up the internal phone to Alan, our administrator on HLC, and asked him, "Please arrange for one of the water tankers already bringing water to Hong Kong to come to our island." I am glad to say that he did so promptly.

We were allowed only ten minutes running water a day, which meant that we left all our taps turned on and plugs in our baths to capture all the water whenever it came on. I wrote:

> *Caroline is as much of a 'pickle' as ever. She is always into mischief. She loves playing with water – when there is some to play with. One day, she climbed into the bath fully clothed – where all our precious water is stored! She enquired, "Is there water in England?!"*

During this great shortage of water, every drop was saved. Waste water from the washing up went on our garden plants; but many, of course, died. The winter rains failed again that year, and the drought continued. In Hong Kong there were standpipes where water could be obtained only by filling buckets, and there were a lot of arguments among those queuing to fill up their containers. It was a very, very difficult time for us all.

Our three children on HLC

Finally, the rains came in the summer of 1964. Timothy by then was an active, small boy, and always on the move. However, when the first rains came, he stood at our front door looking through the mosquito netting and watched the first rain he had ever seen cascading down on the steep path into our house. He stood still for half an hour, and he had never done that before in his life!

In the hospital, during the drought, tendon graft operations (which required many laundered towels) could not be done. However, Stewart devised an operation to remove the large ulcers that occur on the soles of the feet of many leprosy patients after they lose feeling in their feet. Because many leprosy patients are poor and walk barefoot, the ulcers develop as they walk on rough ground. These are very infected ulcers, and the operation required few laundered towels. He narrowed the foot by removing dead bones, cut out the ulcer and sewed the skin together. With special shoes, the patients were able to walk without getting an ulcer again. When we visited the island in 1973 we met a patient on whom Stewart had done this operation. He told Stewart that his foot was still absolutely fine, but his other foot now had an ulcer and "no-one [had] bothered to operate on that foot!"

On one memorable occasion, in November 1963, we were privileged to receive an invitation to have lunch with the Governor of Hong Kong, in his mansion on Hong Kong Island. His wife had a keen interest in our leprosy work and had visited our island. My problem was to know what to wear and how to organise transport. I was still feeding Timothy and so could not leave him for too long.

Again the Police Post came to our aid. We went in their speedboat, and they intercepted one of the ferries that travelled between a nearby island and Hong Kong. I was wearing a slim-fitting skirt, high heeled shoes and a hat, but I had to jump from the police boat onto the ferry in mid-ocean. This aroused much interest among the other passengers on the ferry, who were all Chinese. Stewart was behind me to check I didn't fall into the sea!

The Governor's house had a big garden and a lovely view over the harbour; and he and his wife were very welcoming. We did not know any of the other guests, because we lived on our remote island, but it was a pleasant occasion and the food was delicious. When the dessert arrived – crème brulée – the caramel over the top was much too hard, and everyone was having difficulty breaking into it. I was sitting on the Governor's right, and he suddenly realised the problem. He picked up his spoon and advised us all to give the caramel a sharp tap. Caramel bits flew everywhere, but no one felt awkward. When we were leaving, the Governor asked us if we had a car, and we said, "No." So he offered us his official Governor's car, a Rolls Royce, to take us down to catch the ferry. We felt very 'posh' driving down in the Governor's limousine to the quay.

When we were living in Hong Kong, there was a small area in the middle of Kowloon call the 'Walled City'. For some historical reason this area remained out of control of the British authorities who ruled Hong Kong at the time. It was near the airport and was approached by going behind a row of shops. There were only very narrow passages with a central drain, down which sewage flowed. There was no law and order. The criminal Chinese 'triads' ruled it, and no one felt safe. We had come to know a Christian couple who had been working in this area very bravely for several years, and they agreed to take us into a small area of the Walled City. It was a scary experience, as every other house was either a gambling den or used for drugs, or a brothel, and we were careful not to step into the central sewer.

A few years later a brave, young English woman, Jackie Pullinger, started Christian work in the Walled City, and Stewart met her on one of his later visits to Hong Kong and prayed with her. In due course, the Walled City was taken over by law and order, and is now a different place altogether.

The first half of 1964 passed quickly, with the usual wide range of activities and responsibilities for Stewart. Parties of visitors would come unannounced, such as the Royal Navy Commodore of Hong Kong who arrived with six senior officers one day. Another day, fifty-five nurses and three doctors from a hospital in Hong Kong had to be shown round. Stewart spoke at meetings in Hong Kong and was happy to educate as many people as possible that leprosy can be cured and that healed patients should be welcomed back into society.

By the middle of 1964, we had been away from England for four years, and it was customary for overseas workers to have home leave for a year after this length of time. Our plane was due to leave on July 9th, and we would stay in Hong Kong for two nights before that. On the Sunday before we left, we went for the last time to The Lord is Willing Church. One of Jean's best friends had visited Jerusalem a year previously and had sent us a wooden cross carved in Jerusalem. Although this was a very precious possession, we presented it to

Pastor Gia for the new church that was being built. The Chinese staff entertained us at a nice leaving party and gave us two pairs of special chopsticks carved with the characters of our Chinese names. We said goodbye to the special patients whom we had got to know best, including Mr Wong. All the things that we would not need in England, including most of our books, we packed carefully in two trunks, and our crockery in a crate, and left them on HLC.

On the long flight from Hong Kong there were no problems, apart from keeping three small children happy. The girls were very good, and little Timothy walked up and down the aisle making friends with everyone. Those were the days when there was space in the aisles on aeroplanes. We made a brief stop in Bahrain, and then flew on to London – finally back in England again! Looking back on our three years in Hong Kong, we realised that in spite of frustrations and difficulties, it was satisfying to know that great steps forward had been made for leprosy sufferers on the island and worldwide; and we were greatly privileged to work with Christian Chinese and see the power of Jesus our Saviour bringing peace and happiness to so many patients.

CHAPTER FIVE

In England 1964-67; the direction of our lives changes dramatically as Stewart studies Microbiology.

*I*t felt cold arriving in England after the heat of Hong Kong. Stewart's parents met us and kindly accommodated us in their home in St Leonards-on-Sea, Sussex to begin with. Their house was spacious and had enough bedrooms for us all. However, it was a huge adjustment and a difficult one. Our initial concern was of course for our children. England was very different for them – so many more people, including doting grandparents. The food was quite different, and they had to get used to going upstairs, something we did not do in our HLC bungalow. After experiencing the lengthy drought in Hong Kong I was constantly turning off taps to use only a minimum of water, as I was appalled at the waste. I also remember sitting on the pebbled beach at Hastings on an August day and hearing Caroline's little voice saying, "Mummy, when is it going to be summer?" The weather was a far cry from Hong Kong's sunshine, sandy beaches and warm blue seas.

For Stewart, it was also not easy living with our family of five in his parents' house. For example, making sure that when the children woke early they did not disturb his parents. Timothy was a happy toddler, always active in some way. We were waiting for Bruce to be born at the end of September or early October. I went to see our doctor to check all was well with my pregnancy. He asked if this was my first baby and was somewhat surprised to hear it was our fourth!

Ruth started at a lovely little nursery school called Stonecourt, which was run by an order of Anglican nuns. She was a solitary little girl to begin with, as she'd lived on a relatively deserted island and was not accustomed to the company of other children. On Hay Ling Chau, there had been only one other family with two small girls. Later, Caroline joined Ruth at Stonecourt School, and they were both happy there.

Bruce was born on a stormy night on the last day of September. He was a small baby under six pounds but very healthy, and the nurses called him 'Baby Doll'. He was a cheerful, lively little baby and after a while slept in the same room as Caroline, who was brilliant at entertaining him in the early mornings when he woke up, to keep him from waking the rest of us up.

It became increasingly clear that we needed to find our own house to live in. Kind though the Goodwin grandparents were, there were inevitable frictions. In November 1964, we found a fully furnished house just up the road from Stewart's parents' house. It had three stories, spacious reception rooms downstairs, a large kitchen, seven bedrooms and a nice garden, which was a source of great joy. I remember well the large, red poppies. However, our salary from The Leprosy Mission was remarkably small – just £120 a month.

Fortunately, my parents had sold their home, and they were happy to join us, helping with the rent and expenses. My mother was particularly good with young children. We moved there ten days before Christmas. We were also able to accommodate my two older brothers during holiday times; they were both schoolmasters. After Christmas, my sister and her family visited us, so that we were thirteen for lunch. Unexpectedly, we stayed in that house for eighteen months and had a large number of visitors.

As it was an old house with open fireplaces, we advertised for a cleaner/helper. On the Monday morning after the advertisement, at 9:00 a.m. sharp, a wonderful cockney lady arrived on the doorstep. She stayed with us all the time we were in the house. We certainly could not have done without her. Sixteen months later, when we were due to buy our own house and needed to buy furniture, she came with me to auctions in Hastings and would indicate whether an item was worth buying. We were a busy household. Once a week, a pleasant woman who was a competent cook came to bake for us. She had a marvellous light touch with pastry and taught Caroline that art, which we still enjoy each Christmas with Caroline's mince pies.

The Leprosy Mission relied on donations from Christians in churches for its income for all its work and salaries. So when overseas workers, such as Stewart, returned from abroad, they were happy to tell the supporters of their work among leprosy patients. A large number of talks and sermons were arranged for him around England, Northern Ireland and in Dublin. He told people about his discovery of reversing leprosy nerve damage and his operations on faces, how healed leprosy patients were being rehabilitated back into society and how Jesus Christ was welcomed as Saviour and Lord by Indians and Chinese. In fact, Jesus seemed to be more real to such people in their need than to comparatively well-off Westerners.

While Stewart was away, it was fortunate for me that I had the support of my parents and the others who helped me. In early January 1965, we were preparing for Bruce to be baptised. Various friends and relatives came to the baptism, and we were glad that my father's twin sisters were able to be with us. A Bart's nursing friend of mine was Bruce's godmother; and a friend of Stewart's – an Anglican clergyman, who later became a bishop – was Bruce's godfather. I was very happy that my father took the service and baptised our youngest child. Then on January 15th it was the Golden Wedding anniversary of my parents, who had been married in West China in 1915. We had a wonderful celebration.

During February, Caroline and Timothy both caught measles badly. They had to sleep in a darkened room with the steam kettle going continuously to ease their chest symptoms. Our GP was a kind and experienced doctor. It was most reassuring to have his expert care. Ruth then succumbed to a severe attack of mumps, and Bruce also had a minor attack.

In between his speaking engagements, Stewart started to write his Doctor of Medicine thesis for Cambridge University, and completed it in the summer. The 176 pages included his discovery that the lining of the nose is the primary source of infection in leprosy. For every doctorate for a university degree there is a requirement for an oral examination. However, if the standard of the thesis is considered to be high enough, Cambridge allowed the degree to be awarded as a 'Dissertation' without the need for this oral examination. In due course, Stewart received a telephone call from Cambridge saying that the reviewing committee considered his thesis to be of a high enough standard to warrant a Dissertation. We thanked God very much for that. He bought a second-hand, all-scarlet Cambridge MD gown and hood, which he would use later when he lectured around the world and in universities.

Normally, when Christian workers such as us come home after four years' work, they return to their work after one year. As we expected to return to Hong Kong after a year in England, we had left our few trunks and other belongings packed up in our house on the leprosy island. However, in the summer of 1965, disturbing news came from The Leprosy Mission. Stewart had been specifically trained in leprosy surgery, but the Australian surgeon on HLC did not see the need for another surgeon on the island. Of course, this was a severe shock to us, as we had learnt the Cantonese language specifically so that we could continue working in Hong Kong. We had got to know the staff and leprosy patients, and had left most of our belongings there. So we had to write to the island administrator and ask him to put our luggage on a ship back to England.

At the end of June, Stewart saw the Chairman of the Mission and was told that while the Mission looked for somewhere else for him to work they would pay for him to do any postgraduate medical training course in England. Among many possible courses, Stewart found that the Diploma in Bacteriology (Dip Bact) sounded the most interesting, and it lasted for only one year; but he had to apply soon, as the course started in October. The Diploma qualified a doctor to work as a Hospital Microbiologist and was an intensive course on all human diseases caused by microbes. It was highly sought after by Microbiologists from all over the world, and only sixteen doctors were on the course. Incidentally, if Stewart achieved this degree, it would greatly widen any future job prospects and affect every aspect of our family life. However, when Stewart made enquiries, he found there was no vacancy for the course starting in October.

In the middle of September, Stewart and I took Ruth and Caroline to London for their first visit there. We enjoyed seeing the Changing of the Guard in Horse Guards Parade, and Buckingham Palace. However, our minds were in turmoil; we wondered whether we should resign from The Leprosy Mission and whether Stewart should become a family doctor (General Practice) in England. There was a vacancy for such a post in the beautiful village of Sedlescombe in the country behind Hastings and St Leonards, so we all went there for a good look. However, after much prayer, we decided that this was not the right decision for us at that time.

First, we decided to see if there were any other openings in leprosy work. There was a vacancy at a big Government leprosy hospital in Eastern Nigeria called Uzuakoli. So on a memorable day, October 1st, 1965, Stewart took his application for the post of Leprosy Physician at Uzuakoli to London. However, when he got to the Nigerian Embassy it was closed, as it was a public holiday in Nigeria, their Independence Day, and there was nowhere to leave his letter. Two years later, we realised that if we had gone to Eastern Nigeria, which later declared itself Biafra, we would have been in the middle of a fierce civil war; and with our young family our lives would have been at risk, and we would certainly have faced starvation!

That October day was a Friday afternoon, and Stewart knew that he was not far from the London School of Hygiene and Tropical Medicine in Gower Street, where he had done some studies before we went to India. The Dip Bact course was taught in their fine Microbiology Department.

Stewart walked to the School, went to the office of the Secretary of the Professor of Microbiology and started chatting. He discovered that the next course was due to start on the following Monday. So he said to her, "It is stupid to ask, but I wonder if there is any vacant place on that course?"

To his great astonishment, the secretary said, "We have just had a telegram today from India saying that the two Indian Microbiologists, who were due to come on the course, have cancelled their places because of the new war that has just started between India and Pakistan. They are not permitted to come and join the course."

Stewart's mouth dropped open, and he said, "Well, I should be delighted to join the course, if I'm considered sufficiently experienced."

The secretary said, "I will have to ask the Professor."

Stewart immediately went to a telephone box (no mobile phones in those days) and phoned The Leprosy Mission. They agreed to pay for the course and his daily travel to London, and to continue his small salary.

Early the next Monday morning, I answered the telephone and heard the words, "This is Professor Evans from the Diploma in Bacteriology Course in London. Is Goodwin there?" I explained to him that my husband was taking our two little daughters to nursery school, but would be back soon. "Tell him to ring me when he returns," said the Professor. When Stewart returned, I gave him the message, and he immediately phoned the Professor.

The conversation was very short. Professor Evans said, "Goodwin, you did Part II Pathology at Cambridge, didn't you?"

Stewart replied, "Yes."

"Well, come this afternoon and join the course".

What an unexpected opportunity!

At Cambridge University, if a student has compressed the normal preclinical three year course into two years and passed the final exams, then during the third year they can study any subject. Stewart had achieved this and chose to do Part II Pathology, which included more advanced microbiology. So he had a much greater knowledge of microbiology than most doctors. We thanked God for this amazing development, and it totally changed the rest of our life and that of our family. Until June 1966, Stewart took the 7:45 a.m. train every morning from Hastings to London. It was during this time that Timothy (now eighteen months old) used to wake early and urgently demanded that Dad read him a story before he left for the train! I continued with our family life, and it was a great help to have my parents with us, and also my brothers during the holidays.

We did not go back to Hong Kong, and much later we learnt of the problems that schooling caused for the other family on the leprosy island. Their two young girls went to school in Hong Kong, but the island was far away from Hong Kong and the school. With their mother they had to live in Hong Kong, while their father had to live on HLC from Monday to Friday. Stewart and I would have hated that arrangement, and realised that God had ordered our lives in the best way for us.

In January 1966, snow arrived in our garden, the first that our children had experienced. Towards the end of January, we were told by The Leprosy Mission that our luggage from Hong Kong had arrived at the Headquarters in London. However, when Stewart opened the crate, he found the trunks were not ours but belonged to another family in The Leprosy Mission! In due course our luggage did arrive, and we were reunited with our personal possessions. Unfortunately, the trunk in which our books had been packed was not made of good material and had a slight crack in the bottom. The intense humid heat of Hong Kong had got into the trunk, and by the time it was sent to England most of our precious books had rotted!

We were praying very much that the Mission would find a suitable place for us and our four children. About that time, The Leprosy Mission had just agreed to be a major partner in a big new leprosy project in Ethiopia, based at an existing hospital on the outskirts of the capital Addis Ababa, where patients were treated by Government staff. The project was the 'All Africa Leprosy and Rehabilitation Training Centre' (ALERT). Doctors and paramedical staff would come from all over Africa and would be taught by newly appointed ALERT staff on how to treat patients in the best way.

The Mission asked us if we were prepared to go to Ethiopia, where Stewart would be the main ALERT doctor teaching in the wards and outpatient clinics of the hospital, and might be required to help out treating patients in the hospital. One other doctor would be in charge of the outpatient clinics in the countryside around Addis Ababa, and teaching in these clinics. As we had prayed that the Mission would find the right place for us, we concluded this was God's will. We had no idea how our future would work out, but we were confident that God would arrange our lives for us and our children. Our family have called this 'embracing the unexpected'! Little did we know that in Ethiopia the leprosy hospital was a short driving distance from a fine Christian American day-school, to which Ruth and Caroline could go, while Timothy and Bruce could go to schools in the city of Addis Ababa.

The next shock that came to us was when Stewart learnt that after the academic Dip Bact course he must do a year's clinical microbiology work in a hospital in England, to get experience in infectious diseases and laboratory tests in patients. This would start in the summer of 1966 and be a normal paid post. We explained this to the Mission and were relieved that they agreed that we could delay our departure for Ethiopia until the summer of 1967.

As Stewart had never worked in a junior capacity in a hospital microbiology laboratory, it was unlikely he would get a middle-grade post in a hospital, which would be appropriate for a Dip Bact graduate. The only other place to train in clinical microbiology was in one of the several laboratories of the Public Health Laboratory Service (PHLS). In many large cities, the PHLS provided microbiology services for the city hospitals, and public health expertise for the local community. The Director of the PHLS was Sir James Howie, and his deputy was Dr Jos Kelsey, a committed Christian.

It was rather remarkable that when Stewart was a medical student he had lived in a hostel next to the house where Jos lived and had got to know him well. He went to see Jos and asked what sort of job might be available for him.

Jos said, "If you work in the PHLS for only a year, we will have to employ you as a holiday relief in different laboratories for three months at a time."

Stewart replied, "We have four young children, and we can't keep moving around."

Jos said, "There is an alternative. If you resign from The Leprosy Mission and become a permanent member of the PHLS, you will work in one laboratory and we will guarantee that in 1967 you are transferred to The Leprosy Mission for two years' work in Ethiopia. When you return to England you will go back to the same post in our laboratory."

Stewart replied, "But we intended to work in The Leprosy Mission for all our lives."

Jos said, "Why don't you go home, discuss it with Jean and pray about it."

Stewart and I did indeed discuss it and prayed a lot, as this would totally re-orientate our lives. We were doubtful that the Mission would allow us to resign but be seconded to Ethiopia for two years. With much trepidation we did ask them, and much to our astonishment they agreed! Stewart had an interview with Sir James Howie, who offered him a remarkably senior post as one of two 'Senior Registrars' in the large PHLS microbiology laboratory in Portsmouth. Stewart then had an interview with the Director of the Portsmouth Laboratory who kindly agreed to appoint him – also, that Stewart would be seconded in 1967 to The Leprosy Mission in Ethiopia for two years and then return to his post in Portsmouth. All that Stewart had to do now was to pass the exam for the Dip Bact –

which he did! His job in Portsmouth would start on September 1st 1966.

We were fortunate to find a suitable house with four bedrooms for sale in the pleasant town of Fareham, not far from Portsmouth; but we only obtained a mortgage because my elder brother Lionel very generously helped us with the deposit. So it was on July 30th that we started living in the first home we owned in England, a new situation for us. There was a lovely large playroom the width of the house, looking straight out onto the garden. We settled in, and Stewart and I learnt a lot about wallpapering and DIY from two nice workmen who helped us with modifications to the house.

I was glad to find that a friend I had met when I was doing secretarial work lived about a hundred yards up the same road from our house. She also had two young daughters, and it was a great pleasure to catch up with her. Ruth and Caroline went to the local junior school, Tim started kindergarten, and Bruce joined a playgroup. All these were within walking distance of our home. We joined a welcoming church, St Johns, with a good Sunday school for our children.

While Stewart was working in the Portsmouth Laboratory, he read a report about a new method of detecting infection in the urine using a plastic 'dip-spoon' containing agar that grew bacteria. Pregnant women get bladder infection but without symptoms, which must be detected because it can affect the baby. However, testing every pregnant woman involved large numbers of specimens. In collaboration with the Renal[15] Unit in Portsmouth, Stewart did a large study of pregnant women using dip spoons, which was far more efficient for the laboratory. He wrote a paper about his work, but it was not published until we were in Ethiopia. When we returned to England, Stewart was pleased to learn that many doctors had requested a copy of the paper. The method has become standard practice throughout England and in many other countries.

With a doctor at the Common Cold Research Unit, Stewart studied methods of detecting the smallest bacteria that cause human infection, the mycoplasmas. One species can cause serious chest infection. He devised a technique to grow this (and other

---

[15] kidney

mycoplasmas), and detected it in Timothy's chest when he had an infection – possibly the first such detection in England! Stewart was also asked to oversee the treatment of a local leprosy patient, an Anglo-Indian, who had many complications.

The countryside behind Fareham included extensive woods where we walked every weekend. We discovered where primroses and violets grew in the spring, and in autumn and winter we found huge fir–cones. Lee–on-Solent was our nearest seaside town, and we would drive down on a Saturday and enjoy the sea breezes. We also explored nearby places such as the New Forest, and one Saturday we went to Winchester and visited the famous cathedral. It was a memorable visit because Bruce (aged two-and-a-half) escaped into a cordoned-off choir area of the cathedral.

A slightly annoyed cathedral steward appeared and asked Stewart if that was his son. Stewart hastily thought up the following: "Yes. His name is Bruce, named after Robert the Bruce, an ancestor of my wife's; William, after William the Conqueror; and Goodwin, after Harold Godwin." (My family tree goes back to before the time of William the Conqueror and includes Robert the Bruce.)

The steward, slightly taken aback, replied, "Maybe he has a right to explore the cathedral!"

We kept two guinea pigs, obtained from Stewart's laboratory in Portsmouth; and we grew strawberries, raspberries and carrots. It was a pleasure to be able to have family and friends to stay. My parents came soon after we moved in. When my parents were with us, my father started the habit of 'wandering'. If he heard the sound of a cricket match being played on a nearby field, he would go off and watch. Unfortunately he could never remember the way home. So our children would take off on their bicycles to find Grandpa. The police also came to his rescue more than once. I would receive a phone call from them: "Mrs Goodwin, we have your father here." We never really lost him, but of course my mother was worried. During our time in Fareham, Stewart's sister Joanna was married from her parents' home in St Leonards. Ruth and Caroline were both lovely-looking little bridesmaids.

That year was a stable time for us, but Ethiopia was going to be our next home. Before we left in 1967, we all had to have vaccine injections against Yellow Fever, and Stewart obtained human serum (immunoglobulin) to protect us against the severe hepatitis prevalent in Ethiopia. We wrote to all our relatives and friends who had been, and would be, praying for us while we were abroad again. We started the letter with a reference to the passage in Acts chapter 8 when Philip met an Ethiopian man:

Philip told him the good news of Jesus.

In our letter we wrote:

We pray that as the Lord leads us to this new land we too may have similar opportunities, and the gospel of Jesus may be the power of God and the salvation to many. We praise God that we have had wonderful fellowship, and opportunities to talk about Jesus and the Gospel here in Fareham and Portsmouth. Jean has spoken to Young Wives groups; some women were quite challenged! We are now booked to fly on September 19th, arriving at Addis Ababa the next morning.

During June we have to buy clothes and shoes for all of us for two years, because we gather that ready-made things are expensive in Addis. We will rent out our house here while we are away. We thank God for gifts of money that have come unexpectedly and which seemed to come just when the housekeeping money was running out. Our way is now charted to Ethiopia, that rather backward land of vast mountains and valleys, and an ancient, fossilised Coptic Church. As we all six are about to live in yet another country (our fourth!) we do want to emphasise that we depend on and value your prayers for us, for strength and wisdom in our day-to-day life and happiness for our children settling into new schools. Initially there will be problems of acclimatisation due to the high altitude of Addis, so please pray for our health.

At that time, the Suez Canal was closed because Israel and Egypt had been at war. So our luggage had to be sent round the African Cape arriving at Djibouti, from where the bags went by train to Addis Ababa. We packed up our crockery and household possessions, sent them off, and all boarded the plane for Ethiopia.

Jean Goodwin

CHAPTER SIX

Ethiopia in 1967 – still a wild country; our last two years of leprosy work.

&thiopia was a closed book for us. When we were there, Emperor Haile Selassie was the absolute ruler. He was small in stature but had an impressive personality. His granddaughters – Ethiopian princesses – had been at the same school as I had in England, and one had become quite a good friend of mine. She was very kind to us while we were in her country. Her family were part of the Amhara tribe, who also provided the rulers of the various provinces and were dominant in the capital, Addis Ababa. Amharas were not dark skinned and had aquiline features. Some were tall, and many women strikingly beautiful. In this land of mountain ranges and isolated deep valleys were many different tribes, with sixty different languages.

In the north of the country is the source of the Blue Nile river; in the west, Nilotic tribes live along the White Nile; and in the south many tribes were in constant conflict with each other, and most lived in primitive conditions. When we were in Ethiopia it was markedly undeveloped – only 1% of the population could read. A doctor who drove out of Addis for only two hours on his first visit to a country clinic was surprised that the local villagers brought grass to his car! They assumed all means of transport needed such 'food'. They had never seen a car before that day. The centre of Addis Ababa appeared to be that of a modern city, but the outskirts rapidly merged into traditional countryside with bullocks pulling ploughs, and women carrying large pots of water or loads of firewood on their backs. Donkeys were the sole means of transport for the village people who

brought their goods into the city. Huge eucalyptus trees lined the roads and grew on the hills surrounding the city. They were most impressive but were not native to Ethiopia. They had been brought from Australia and were useful for firewood.

The Ethiopian Orthodox Church was dominant, with monasteries and churches spread out across the northern part of the country, but its teachings were based more on the importance of saints and less on the New Testament.[16] The people were conscious of evil spirits and their power; and their beliefs and customs mixed superstition and Christianity. In the vehicle that took us from the airport was a fine Ethiopian man, who asked Stewart the existential question, "Why is sin in Christianity often referred to as 'black'?" Stewart was able to reassure him that the Bible says, "Though your sins are scarlet, they shall be white as snow."[17] This challenging question launched us into our two-year stay in Ethiopia.

Addis Ababa is situated a at height of 7600 feet; this makes people breathless for the first two weeks, and so we were advised to rest for an hour after lunch every day. During this time, we stayed at a guest-house run by the Mennonite Church of America. They were kind and hospitable, and we were well looked after there.

The first night we were woken by loud rustling sounds and 'barking' just outside our bedrooms. In the morning we asked, "What was that sound we heard?"

We were told, "Oh, those are hyenas around the garbage bins!"

This showed how the countryside came right into the city.

ALERT was based in an older hospital in a rural area on the edge of Addis – the Princess Zenebework Hospital. This was the Government leprosy hospital, with one elderly English doctor (Margaret) and Ethiopian nurses. Usually, a leprosy hospital is sited well away from a town. So we were fortunate that the hospital was not too far from shops and schools.

---

[16] Even at the time of writing, in 2012, most priests do not own a Bible.
[17] Isaiah chapter 1

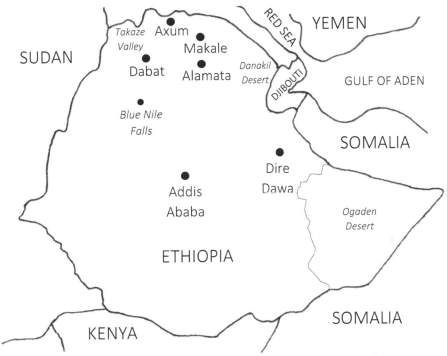

The main hospital building was an old two-storey structure, and longer-term patients were housed in four simple wooden buildings in the grounds. There was a large clinic for treating leprosy foot ulcers, and special shoes were made for them. It was planned that the doctors brought in by the ALERT project would do more training and lecturing than routine work; but soon after we arrived, Margaret developed severe heart trouble, and so Stewart had to do virtually all the hospital work (wards and clinics), as well as his ALERT work.

Plans were being made to build a big new hospital, and while we were there the Emperor laid the foundation stone for it.

When we arrived, houses for staff had not yet been built in the hospital grounds. So our first house was about half a mile away from the hospital, surrounded by fields and down a rough track. The walk to and from the hospital was good exercise for Stewart, but he was glad of a stout stick to ward off the wild dogs. Our house had a tall fence surrounding the garden and house; and for our safety, we had to have a day guard and a night guard. Our day guard was a young man called Hussein who had grown up in a remote rural area without any education. He came to us with orange hair, as he had been malnourished; but after a few months on a better diet his hair changed to a black colour. He did not know about a normal house, even how to open doors. In the Ethiopian countryside everyone lived in round mud houses with a single room and a thatched roof (called a 'tukul'), and just a curtain across the doorway. After we moved to a house in the hospital grounds in May 1968, he stayed with us, and throughout the rest of our two years in Ethiopia. Our night guard was called Zaudi – a likeable rogue who knew the local thugs and robbers, and therefore we hoped he would keep them away. I came home one evening to find Hussein and Zaudi having a fight. It was necessary to take immediate action and intervene to avoid them causing each other serious damage. I shouted at them, "Stop that at once!" and was very relieved when they did so. After that, I made sure that their duty times did not overlap much. We also needed a large dog to guard our house, and soon after moving in, we were very fortunate to hear of an Alsatian dog that needed a home; 'Lily' was a lovely animal. One memorable night, we were surrounded by robbers, but Lily and Zaudi kept them away. Later we heard that those robbers had been caught and all hanged at the scene of their crime, as was the punishment at the time. We were relieved that they were not hanged near our house.

A Ford Taunus estate car was provided by ALERT for our use. I used it every day to take the children to school and do the shopping. It was not a four-wheel drive but had front-wheel drive – a help on the gravel roads in the countryside, 'pulling' the car round hair-pin bends, which were numerous up and down the mountains. We soon learnt that you should never brake on a corner but beforehand. In a front-wheel drive, if one brakes on a corner, the back wheels will slide away and you will go over the edge, which on Ethiopian country roads was often a steep drop! We had not driven on the right hand side of the road before, and we would also have to get used to the Ethiopian traffic. I met an Ethiopian lady and was explaining to her that I was worried about the driving, and immediately she offered to come with me initially, until I was more accustomed to it. When we reached the first roundabout, none of the cars waited for other cars. How would I join the traffic?

I said to her, "What do I do?"

She said, "Just go."

So I did! I soon got used to the lack of 'rules of the road' and thanked God that I never had an accident or even a near miss. In November 1967 I wrote:

> *Driving in Addis is a nightmare – people, donkeys, cows, sheep, potholes, and cars – all in the road, with no traffic sense. It's awful. We do need prayer constantly for protection on the roads and from harming people or animals. There are a lot of hyenas that we hear in the ravines around the road near the hospital. So we pray we don't break down. The wild dogs make a fantastic din howling at night.*

Eighteen months later I recorded that practically every time I went out I saw an accident of some sort. When it rained it was impossible to know how deep the potholes were. So great caution was needed when driving. I shall never forget returning to our house from the centre of town one morning after heavy rain; the road was full of potholes, and the potholes were full of water. I saw one elderly leprosy patient with his Ethiopian cape[18] wrapped round him, sitting in the road with his large foot ulcer uncovered, carefully washing his bandages in one of the potholes full of water. It was such a sorry sight and enough to make me weep.

It may have been because we lived at a high altitude, but our four children were often ill with fevers, coughs and colds, especially Timothy (aged four). We thanked God that none of us got more serious illnesses like hepatitis, which was common in Ethiopia, probably because Stewart administered an injection of immunoglobulin to us every eight months. In our home, we employed an Ethiopian woman called Yadjebush as cook and occasional childminder. She was a lovely lady and became indispensable. Before coming to us, she had worked with a Swedish family and could speak Swedish but not English. I found myself talking Chinese to her, as I

---

[18] 'shamma'

knew I had to use a non-English language, but when she replied in Swedish there was some confusion! Guidebooks we had read stated that there were no poisonous snakes in Ethiopia, but the first time we drove into the hospital grounds a bright green snake slithered across the road in front of us. The bright green colour showed it was a bamboo snake – and very poisonous! Our first house had a wooden rail by the side of the front steps, with a creeper growing up the rail and onto the verandah around the house. One evening, we saw a black snake slithering across the floor of our living room. After we killed it, Stewart took it to an English doctor who had worked in Nigeria, and he immediately identified it as a poisonous 'night adder'. We immediately cut down the creeper around the house. The next evening we were hosting a prayer meeting in our living room. While everyone was praying, Stewart and I kept our eyes open, not shut!

There was only one Western-type supermarket in Addis, and the price of Western foods was three times higher than in England. However, our salary from The Leprosy Mission was the same as it had been in Hong Kong. So we were grateful for the occasional gift of £20-£100 from Stewart's parents and a few others. Stewart had to ask The Leprosy Mission to cash in all his pension money, so at least we could have enough money to live. Fortunately, the price of petrol was low. I discovered that baking cakes at an altitude of eight thousand feet required adjusting proportions of cooking ingredients; otherwise the cake was a complete failure. After several such disasters, I was shopping one day in the supermarket, when I noticed on the side of a carton of baking flour from the USA, "Recipes for different altitudes". These showed a different proportion of ingredients at sea level, four thousand feet and eight thousand feet. This was a marvellous boon, because I now knew exactly what to do to make delicious cakes at the high altitude at which we lived. I cooked on butane gas, which arrived in cylinders. The altitude meant that only a special grain could be grown – teff – with which Ethiopians made a thick pancake with holes called 'injera'. They broke pieces off and dipped them into the local stew called 'wat'. The market area of the city was the 'Mercato', and in this area almost anything edible could be found, or things like a saucepan or even an exotic scarf. All this added to the spice of life in Addis at the time.

Schools of course were our concern. Bruce (aged three) was too young to go to school at the beginning of our stay. Tim went to a nursery school run by a competent and kind American lady, which he enjoyed. A year later, with much regret, he had to leave that school. He had felt secure and happy. Later, both Tim and Bruce went to a school mainly for Ethiopian children – a round trip of twenty-three kilometres. For Ruth and Caroline (aged eight and six), there was an American Christian School called 'The Good Shepherd', on the outskirts of Addis Ababa, fortunately on our side of the city. They liked the school and benefited from it. Fortunately, we did not need to learn more than a few basic Amharic words. It is a very complicated language, as even a word like 'come' has three variations – male, female and neuter (for an animal).

Living at nearly eight thousand feet could cause physical or mental health problems, and we were advised to spend a day every month at a lower altitude. We discovered a small place 120 km away called Sodere at 4800 feet, right near the large Awash River, where an Olympic-sized swimming pool with hot spring water was being built with small cabins around it. When the pool was nearly completed, the workers awoke one morning to find a crocodile in the swimming pool! Needless to say, a substantial fence was rapidly built around the resort, which also kept out the hippopotami that would leave the river every evening to eat vegetation in the area. We were picnicking there one Saturday, and Ruth was about to eat an apple. As she turned to talk to me, a vervet monkey leapt down from the trees and grabbed it from her hand, much to her annoyance. Sodere is now a big 'spa' centre.

I have been told that I have the 'gift of hospitality'. This is something I enjoy and am able to do. While we were in Addis, Dr Paul Brand, the famous leprosy surgeon, visited ALERT for a while. When we were in India, he had taught Stewart leprosy surgery. In Addis he was on his own, and so we frequently invited him to meals in our home. African doctors and paramedical workers (from other African countries) came to ALERT to study, and Stewart would give them lectures and teach them how to treat all forms of leprosy and its complications. These young men also enjoyed coming to our home. They obviously missed their own families and played with our children. Voluntary Service Overseas young men and women (VSOs) had come from various countries including England and Sweden to work in ALERT. They were always glad of a meal at our house and some home life.

No other hospital in Addis would treat leprosy patients or their families, so Stewart had to cope with all their other illnesses and deliver babies – once by torchlight when the electricity failed. In Stewart's clinic at 8:30 a.m. every morning were new patients to be diagnosed and put on anti-leprosy drug treatment. Some had walked for many weeks over the mountain ranges to get to the leprosy hospital. Then at 11:00 a.m. was the 'sick patients' clinic, where forty patients with every leprosy complication and other diseases (even smallpox) were seen by Stewart and the clinic nurse – a beautiful, calm Ethiopian woman who organised the patients. On a typical day Stewart might see a young man shivering in front of him, with what looked like snowflakes in his hair. Before Stewart examined the patient he realised these were lice, and the man must be suffering from louse-borne relapsing fever. This is usually fatal in a few days and occurs nowhere else but Ethiopia. So he would say to the young man, "I can admit you to hospital, if you let me burn all your clothes and shave your head." This was the only way to prevent lice getting into the hospital and causing disease in other patients. Some patients suffered from eye diseases such as trachoma, and it was fortunate that Stewart had studied eye diseases before we left England in 1960. He also was in charge of the laboratory and published research on leprosy foot ulcers. Occasionally, he had to do emergency operations, such as to release infection in an infected bone, or on eyelids when trachoma caused the eyelashes to turn in and rub against the cornea. In Stewart's diary he recalled a leprosy patient's baby with severe meningitis, whom he was able to cure. However, another baby who had been perfectly well at 8:00 a.m. died a few hours later, and Stewart suspected it had been poisoned by a witch doctor. One young man, called Berhanc, was very ill with severe tuberculosis and amoebic dysentery, as well as leprosy. At the time, Stewart was about to go away for a few days, teaching trainees who had come to

ALERT. On his ward round before he left, he asked Berhane, "Have you understood the Gospel of Jesus?" He replied, "He is my Saviour," and we thank God that in due course he completely recovered.

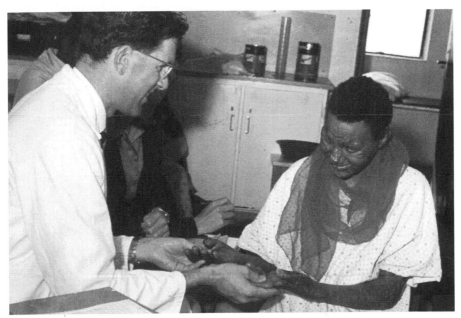

Stewart's Leprosy Clinic

Rabies was common in the wild dogs that roamed everywhere, and so whenever we went for a walk with our family, Stewart would carry a stone, which he would throw to keep a dog with a foaming mouth away from us. Fortunately, when a dog has advanced rabies it is not so active and would often be sitting still. So God protected us all in many ways. We were out for a walk one afternoon – all six of us – when a group of leprosy beggars approached us. When they first saw us they started cringing and holding out their deformed hands for money. Suddenly, these beggars recognised Stewart as 'their doctor'[19] and their smiles and greetings were overwhelming. It was such a heart-warming experience for all of us and especially for our children.

Stewart was walking on the ground floor of the old hospital one day, when he heard a huge crash behind him. It was the lavatory bowl from the ward on the floor above, which had become full of

---

[19] 'hakim'

stones that the patients had used to wipe themselves; this was their custom, as there was certainly no toilet paper and little water in the countryside. Thankfully, the bowl had not fallen on Stewart!

He asked the physiotherapist to treat the many cases of early leprosy nerve damage that he detected, as he had discovered in Hong Kong that such damage could be reversed. The physiotherapist soon realised how effective early intervention was. As Stewart did his ward rounds one day, he noticed a young man trying to lift a glass of water from his bedside locker. He failed to do so because his fingers were so weak. However, after he received Stewart's treatment and physiotherapy, his finger-strength totally recovered; and when we left he was helping to build the new leprosy hospital.

A nasty complication of leprosy causes fever, which is relieved by steroid drugs. However, the fever returns when the steroids are stopped, so patients ended up being given steroids for too long and developed bad side-effects from them. About thirty such patients were referred to Stewart from hospitals around the country. Stewart read about a new anti-inflammatory drug (flufenamic acid) that he thought might replace this steroid treatment. He wrote to the makers in the USA and was very grateful to receive the free gift of a large quantity of the drug. He carefully gave it to his patients and it stopped the fever; he was also delighted to find that the fever did not return when the medication was stopped. However, when he stopped the steroids initially, he had to walk round the wards in the evenings to check that the patient had not developed the possible complication of swelling of the throat that could stop them breathing!

We much enjoyed going to Christ Chapel (American Baptists) on Sundays. It had good teaching and a good Sunday school – Bruce learnt the Lord's Prayer in an American accent. We often entertained the pastor and his wife, and members of the church, especially those in the church choir. We both became members of the choir and enjoyed the practices and singing. In a letter I wrote:

> There was a Parent-Teacher's meeting at Good Shepherd School not long ago. They have a good selection of teachers this year – a number who come to our church and whom we have been happy to meet and make friends with, particularly Jackie and Larry with their four daughters. Jackie is a nurse and is looking after the boarders. I am taking her to the market this coming week.

At Christ Chapel we met Rev. and Mrs James Luckman, who had worked in Ethiopia for many years and spoke the Amharic language (the main language in Addis Ababa) well. They had returned to Addis for a visit. We had been concerned that there was no Christian activity associated with ALERT. It was sad that The Leprosy Mission had signed up to be a partner, without specifying the need for a chaplain in the hospital. Everyone needs help in their body and their soul, and on our leprosy island in Hong Kong, patients loved to hear about Jesus.

So I asked Mr Luckman (who had no car), "If I come and fetch you, would you speak to the patients in the wards about Jesus?"

He replied, "I should be delighted to do so."

The patients loved listening to him, and many of them responded to the timeless message of Jesus and His salvation. One Ethiopian man was a strong character but deformed, and had been very promiscuous. He worked in the hospital and was wonderfully transformed by Jesus. After that, Stewart would often see him encouraging people to come and hear Mr Luckman. One woman patient, Asho Tinga, had come from the desert area of South-East Ethiopia. When she got leprosy, her husband left her and her young son to starve. Fortunately, she got to a small Christian clinic and they treated her leprosy. Unfortunately, she developed severe complications and was then sent to Stewart for him to sort out. He managed to help her, and after several months in hospital she was about to be discharged. She had become a Christian, and just before she went, she tentatively gave Stewart an amazing present. It was a beautifully embroidered text from the Bible in Amharic, which translates, "I can do all things through Him who strengthens me," with the Bible reference, Philippians chapter 4, verse 13. We have no idea how she managed to buy the green and yellow silk thread. She had embroidered the Ethiopian flag at the top and put a wooden piece at each end, which rolled it up. It is now one of our most precious possessions. Considering she had absolutely nothing in the world, it is the most wonderful tribute to what Jesus was doing for her, and a challenge to us all.

Stewart managed to get hold of some Bibles in Amharic. One day he heard rapidly-running feet outside his office and a young male nurse called Demessie knocked urgently on his door. Demessie asked,

"Please, may I have one of the Bibles?" Stewart was delighted to give him one. When he was living with his family in the country, Demessie had become a true believer in Jesus, and as a result his Ethiopian Orthodox parents had made him sleep on the floor by the kitchen fire. Sadly, the Orthodox Church did not have much influence on the immorality that was prevalent, especially among poorer people. Because of their poverty, many families would sell alcohol and run a brothel. Girls as young as ten years old could be married; and because of their malnutrition and resulting poor bone development, childbirth could be very difficult. Great trauma could result to the bladder and lower bowel, leading to a terrible 'fistula'. Two Australian gynaecologists founded a special hospital to treat such women, and it was opened just before we left. It became the world famous 'Fistula Hospital'.

Many expatriates living in Addis were able to fly down to Nairobi for their holidays and visit the game parks in Kenya. However, we never had sufficient money to do that. So in the school holidays we arranged to drive into the vast, untamed Ethiopian countryside, visiting towns and villages, which we really enjoyed. The elderly doctor Margaret had recovered somewhat and was available to work when we wanted to go away on holiday. The tarmac roads out of Addis Ababa ended after fifty kilometres and then deteriorated into rough, dusty and very stony roads. The dust was enveloping, and so overtaking lorries was hazardous. We had some hair-raising experiences, but God kept us safe through them all. Petrol stations were few and far between, and so we always carried a spare can of petrol, as well as two spare tyres and a can of water on our roof rack. School holidays were ideal times to explore this amazing country, which was still 'stuck' in the past, before development occurred in later years.

Our first big trip was to the north of the country, during the Christmas holidays in January 1968. Our plan was to see the Blue Nile Falls, then visit a doctor friend of Stewart's, who was working farther north, on to the ancient capital of Axum, turn south, and then go to a leprosy hospital in the inland city of Dessie for Stewart to help the staff there – a total of more than two thousand kilometres on very rough roads in our little car! As there was no reliable postal service, nor telephones around the country, we gave letters to our daughters in Good Shepherd School to give to children whose Christian worker parents lived on the route we wanted to take. We hoped this would be enough warning for the parents when we descended on them and that they would be able to put us all up for a night or two. We thank God that this indeed happened! We had got to know an Armenian family, who had lived in Addis for thirty years. One of their sons, Jack, aged seventeen, wanted to take the opportunity to see more of Ethiopia, as up to that time it had been too dangerous to travel to the north. So he came with us and was very useful because he knew a lot about cars, of which Stewart was remarkably ignorant. As it turned out, we didn't know how wonderfully his knowledge would help us at a very dangerous moment. His father gave Jack an AK47 rifle for our 'protection', but Stewart said, "Please leave that hidden under a seat, because we don't want to be held up by people trying to get hold of the gun!" As in all our travels around Ethiopia, we always prayed before we set out, and relied on the promise in Psalm 34:7 that "the angel of the LORD encamps around those who fear him, and he delivers them". We thank God so much for His protection.

Overnight in a tukul

It was January 7th, 1968 when all seven of us piled into our little car and set off. We crossed the deep Blue Nile gorge and on the first night slept in a round mud tukul and chatted to our hosts round the fire in the starlight. Living conditions there were primitive, as in the other places we stayed. Cooking was done on a wood-burning stove.

115

Water was obtained from a well, and the only toilet was a wooden hut with a hole in the ground and a wooden seat over it.

The next day as we drove, Jack suddenly shouted to Stewart, "Stop the car!" He had smelled petrol and found that the plastic petrol pipe under the car from the tank had come off – caused by the many stones on the road. Out was pouring all our precious petrol! He immediately mended it. We did have a spare can of petrol, but it might not have been enough to get us to the next petrol station, and Stewart might not have realised what was wrong. So we could have been stranded miles from anywhere with our four small children; we gave many thanks to God that Jack was with us.

Blue Nile Falls

After an overnight stop with some other kind people, we made a trip to the Blue Nile Falls and on the way saw a black and white Geraza (colobus) monkey. These do not have a thumb and only eat leaves, and they do not steal the crops like baboons do; so they are not killed by the local people. After parking the car, we walked across a rickety wooden bridge onto the slippery path to the viewpoint, to see the four separate waterfalls. The crashing water made a loud sound, and the rainbows in the spray were beautiful. The next day in Gondar, the old capital, we visited a church (with ceiling and walls covered with paintings of saints and apocryphal stories) and two castles three hundred years old, built by the Portuguese in 1600 for the Ethiopian Kings.

We then drove north into the Simien Mountains to the small town of Dabat, climbing two thousand feet; there were views of purple, rocky, jagged peaks, including Mount Ras Dashan, fifteen thousand feet – the highest in Ethiopia. Stewart's doctor friend was working there with his wife and two sons among a unique group of Jews, the Falasha, who had lived there probably for thousands of years. Thirty years later they were all airlifted to Israel (where their DNA was found to be ancient Jewish). We had a picnic on the edge of the escarpment, with magnificent views stretching before us down to the Sudan in the distance, and our children enjoyed games with the two boys.

From Dabat, we left the mountains and descended into the very deep Takaze Valley. Descending took ninety minutes, as there were 120 hairpin bends. I sat in the back seat with our four children, and we lurched from side to side. Caroline complained, "Daddy, why can't you drive straight?!" At the bottom of the valley, there were many ancient baobab trees. On the way up, when we stopped the car for a view, Stewart left the engine running so that the fan would cool the engine.

That night we stayed at a remote farm managed by American Christian workers. Until three years ago this road was unsafe for tourists, as brigands robbed everyone at gunpoint; but recently the Emperor had forbidden the import of bullets, so the brigands needed their bullets for self-protection. Every group walking along the road included one man with a rifle. The next day, after going up and down the tops of six mountain ranges, we reached Axum – the capital of the Ethiopian kingdom in 300 AD, and at that time one of the biggest centres of trade in North Africa. Queen Judith had erected huge standing columns or steles with extensive carving – one hundred feet high. The largest one had fallen down, and we were able to appreciate the immense work that had gone into the carving. It has been estimated to weigh 510 tons and when it was erected was probably the largest single standing stone in the world. Nearby was the old church of St Mary of Zion. Similar to other Ethiopian monastic churches, women are not allowed inside. The ancient crowns of Ethiopia are kept here, and women could see them through a grill. On the streets were poorly-clad peasants, and donkeys with goatskins of water on their backs. Dilapidated tukuls were dotted around.

We then turned south to Makale, on the more eastern side of Ethiopia. The road wound down into a vast crater, with hermits' caves in the cliff walls and huge birds (Abyssinian ground-hornbills) in the rich fields on the crater floor. One flat-topped mountain with sheer sides had a male-only monastery that could be reached only with the aid of a rope. The views from the road were dramatic, but there was a very steep drop by the side of the narrow road. Stewart said to me, "I do want to take a photo of this." I replied, "Certainly not! Bruce is only three, and he will want to get out and pretend to take a photo. It's much too dangerous!" We reached Makale as darkness fell, with the full moon lighting our way. We had directions to the home of Irish Christian workers, but as it was so late they had bolted and barred their gates. We had to bang and shout before they believed that we had actually turned up.

The following morning, walking to the market area, we passed trains of camels loaded with large salt blocks brought up from the Danakil Desert, seven thousand lower – the hottest place on earth.

My blonde hair and our white-skinned children attracted much attention, and we were approached by an employee from the one hotel, who asked, "Are you the Goodwins?"

We said, "We are!"

He replied, "Your Princess friend has booked rooms for you at the hotel."

It was a lovely surprise – and we immediately moved there. Makale has a pleasant year-long even temperature of about 75°F (24°C) with little humidity. As we left early the next morning, mist lay below us over the Danakil desert, and a string of camels were silhouetted against the morning sun. We climbed over nine mountain ranges, including a drop of three thousand feet down to the town of Alamata, which involved 112 hairpin bends, many more than 180 degrees. We passed long-horned cattle on the roads, but they were all gone by the time of the terrible Ethiopian Famine in that area in 1983-85.

Stewart had been asked to visit the Leprosy Hospital at the inland town of Dessie, but the way there involved turning west off the main road to Addis onto a minor road that was full of deep potholes and large boulders. Jack got out and walked in front of the car guiding us, as our car was in real danger of coming to grief. The next day, while Stewart advised on the treatment of 'complicated' leprosy cases, the rest of us went for a walk; it was reassuring to have Jack with us. We saw a woman pulping a green plant in the hollow of a rock to make the soapy substance that she would use for washing her clothes. A silversmith was at work in one of the tukuls, using an old goatskin as a pair of bellows for his fire, and another man was weaving on a frame outside his house. The children were delighted to see small lambs only a week old that they could pick up, as well as some brown hens. After two nights there, we took the road back to Addis, travelling up to eleven thousand feet in dense mist (driving very slowly) then through three tunnels, and finally we came down into the sun. It was on January 18th at 6:50 p.m. that we arrived at our home near the hospital to find Yadjebush and Hussein waiting for us. There had been three robberies nearby, but our large dog had kept the robbers away from our house. We were happy but tired, and thanked God very much for looking after us – on a road that in 2012 was featured in a BBC television programme as still one of the "The worst journeys in the world"!

One Saturday we were invited to the Emperor's Palace in the centre of Addis, where he had a large zoo. We saw his cheetahs and were able to stroke them. Taking photographs, we were told to keep a watchful eye on the cheetah's tail, which twitched when it was getting cross. I wrote in a letter:

> In the palace grounds are cages with male and female lions, and the male gave a great display of roaring for us! Also, Canadian black bears given to the Emperor, Geraza monkeys, antelope and a large tortoise.

On a weekend in October 1968, we drove south from Addis Ababa to the town of Jimma, which was known for the intricate carved chairs and stools made in that area, carved out of a single tree trunk. They were not expensive, so we bought two stools and a chair. In Jimma, we stayed for a night with Christians who worked among the small Jinjarro tribe, and they told us of thrilling conversions to Christianity. I wrote in a letter:

> One witch doctor had three snakes – pythons – as his companions, and had to put out food for thirty-three spirits every day. He was amazingly converted to faith in Jesus and the next day killed his three pythons with a spear. The local Christians from this tribe wished to challenge the deep superstition around them by using, for their church building, wood from a sacred forest where no one ventured except to sacrifice to the spirits. When the Christians went to cut down the trees, the animists took sacrifices to placate the spirits; but of the three animists who went, two died mysteriously within six days and the third died three months later. Christians began to farm in previously sacred areas; but when the animists tried to plough in that area, all their oxen died. It was revealing to meet these brave people, in the forefront of the battle against Satanic power.

Another Saturday[20] was very memorable. With an American Army Captain friend, we all went for a picnic near the Awash river, at a site which Stewart had noticed on our drive to Jimma as a possible place where very ancient 'people' had lived. Sure enough, on the vertical side of a dry riverbed, human-type bones and small flints were sticking out. There was no notification that this was an official site where antiquities might be found and no warning that any item found there could not be removed. A few young Ethiopian boys were standing around, and one of them was holding what Stewart recognised as an ancient 'hand-axe'. He paid a small price for it. In his diary he wrote "? 2 million years old", but we never met anybody in Addis who knew about such antiquities. Parliamentary legislation forbidding the export of such antiques had not been introduced in Ethiopia before we left in 1969. When we left the country we meticulously obtained export permission for a small lion-skin cushion and a Geraza monkey-skin, but knew of no restriction on the hand-axe. In 2008, Stewart took the hand-axe to the British Museum, and was told it was indeed between 1.2 and 1.6 million years old, made by *Homo ergaster* (the African form of *Homo erectus*) from whom

---

[20] 2nd November 1968 in Stewart's diary

Homo sapiens originated! It has proved to be of great interest to our grandchildren. Apparently, during 1969 the Emperor had made a decree prohibiting the export of such antiquities, but the legislation was not introduced until after we left.

In the autumn of each year, there was an Ethiopian Orthodox 'Maskal' celebration ("Finding of the True Cross") held in the centre of Addis Ababa. Tiers of seats were erected for the large number of people viewing the parade. Tribal chieftains from the rural and tribal areas proudly marched in front of their Emperor, wearing spectacular headgear made of lion skins, and some were *covered* in lion skins; and they all carried long spears. There was even a small flat-bed trailer that carried a lion, only attached by a chain. We trust it was well fed and had no need to sample any members of the crowd for its evening meal! In the middle of the area was an enormous bonfire, with sparks that shot up into the evening air.

Ethiopian Orthodox festival

English and Americans in Addis Ababa enjoyed camping beside Lake Langano – a salt lake within driving distance south of Addis. We did not have the right equipment; for one weekend we thought we would try it, but survived only twenty-four hours before returning home. Nearby was Lake Shalla, which was even more salty than Langano. On the edge of the lake we saw hot springs coming through the earth and on the lake a flock of flamingos, which can tolerate the saltiness and even obtain their food from such waters. A favourite day trip was to drive to a swimming pool in the small town of Ambo, about an hour's drive west of Addis. We had friends from our church there, and the town had a large, heated swimming pool where Caroline learnt to swim.

By May 1968, the staff houses near the hospital were finally finished, in a 'staff only' area. We moved into one of them, with two other families (each with four small children) in houses alongside us. There we were able to grow flowers as well as vegetables in our garden. In a letter I wrote:

> There are eucalyptus woods behind our house, just over the fence. Stewart has made a ladder, which enables him to go with the children into the woods, but not too far!

The family in Ethiopia

We were not allowed to keep our large dog but acquired a small Pekinese-type dog from our Armenian friends; 'Perky' gave our family a lot of pleasure. Sadly, just before we left Addis in 1969, Perky was bitten by a snake in our garden and died. Hussein hunted around in the vegetable patch and found a nest of cobras. We were glad he found them before they found us or our children. Because Yadjebush was happy to 'child-sit' in the evenings for us, we were able to go out to some films and evening activities at our church. However, we obeyed the golden rule in Addis that when you park your car in the evening in the city, you always pay a small boy to stand by the car and prevent petrol being siphoned out from your tank.[21]

Several children of the other two families went to the same school as Tim and Bruce – in fact a total of eight (aged three to five), which filled our estate car. We mothers took it in turn to ferry the children to and from school. One day I was driving home from Addis with the small children in our car, when I got a puncture – a not infrequent experience. When I stopped, the car was immediately surrounded by a group of Ethiopian boys all wanting to change the tyre for me, knowing that I'd have to pay them. So I had to have a clear routine. First I got the children out of the car and told them, "Stand by the side of the road; hold hands and don't move!" Then I had to choose two responsible-looking boys and supervise them, getting the spare tyre out of the back of the car and changing the tyre – quite a feat. Then I got the little ones back into the car safely and found the money required to give to the two boys who had done a good job, remembering which ones they were in the sea of black faces. Finally, I got into the car, started the engine, wound down the window, gave the money to the two boys, and immediately drove off, to avoid the clamour from the other boys for money.

Each November there was an appropriate British 'Remembrance Day' gathering in the pleasant gardens of the British Embassy. It was nice to dress up in our smartest clothes and mingle with the other British people in Addis whom we rarely met.

In December 1968, I wrote to Stewart's parents:

Last Tuesday, the Christmas meeting of our church women's group was in our home, with thirty-five people here. Stewart showed slides of Hong Kong and our leprosy work there. I decorated the sitting-room with our Chinese things, made mince pies, and we had Christmas music on a tape. We sang a few carols and had a short Christmas meditation. I was wearing my Chinese 'pyjama' suit, on which I was complimented. On Thursday we had our choir practice for our Christmas Cantata. Stewart leaves on the 16th and is away teaching the Rural Area

---

[21] During the Ethiopian famine, when our daughter Ruth was working there, one helicopter with aid-workers on board crashed soon after take-off because its fuel had been replaced by water.

Trainees for a whole week. It is a shame that he has to be away
when the children have their Christmas programmes at school.

On the Red Sea coast of Ethiopia at that time was the Port of Assab, on the edge of the Danakil desert – now it is in Eritrea. We decided to go to swim there in the winter holidays – in January 1969 – because in the summer it is one of the hottest places on earth and very humid. We had to drive north from Addis for eighty miles and then turn sharply east towards the Red Sea, off the mountains, to descend to the plains that lead to the coast. The road had many hairpin bends and steep drops by the side where we would see the wrecks of numerous lorries that had left the road and plunged straight down the ravines – a reminder to drive with care! We stopped for the night at the small village of Bati and were kindly put up by Christian workers, with six camp-beds for us. Bati had a big market once a week, to which the Danakil people came up from the plains, and we were there that day. The Danakils are a fierce, proud and spear-carrying tribe who are often at war with each other, and they have a long history of attacking and mutilating the highland Ethiopian men. Most of the women were bare-breasted. On the long drive down to Assab, we passed deep valleys with huge sparkling white salt lakes, because the earth there was below sea level and the sea had penetrated and then evaporated leaving the salt, which looked like snow. The temperature could be above 120°F (47°C) in the shade. In Assab we stayed with German Christians who looked after us well. It was lovely to be by the sea again, with sandy beaches and a warm sea for swimming. This also provided an opportunity to extend my collection of shells. I found many cowrie shells that I still possess. The village of little Assab was quaint, with dusty roads, mud houses, palm trees and donkey carts. At the Sunday evening service, Stewart was asked to give the informal talk. Assab became the main port for the import of grain needed during the Ethiopian famine.

Daily life in our home near the Leprosy Hospital often produced surprises. One day, I noticed a huge stream of soldier ants heading for our front door! I shouted for Hussein, and he said, "I know what to do," and quickly got some branches of eucalyptus leaves. As soon as he put these branches in front of the ants, they diverted away from our house, much to my relief. Apparently no animal, including elephants, will ever face up to soldier ants, usually in their thousands, with their fearsome bites. It would have been devastating if they had invaded our house. One cold winter morning in the school holidays, Stewart was due to fly with a Government health official to a small American Christian hospital in the mountains many miles from Addis, where there were a lot of leprosy patients, and he would have to stay overnight. Travel could either be by Land Rover for ten hours over very rough roads or on a short flight directly from Addis. We decided as a family to all drive with him to the airport and wish him well for his trip. However, the health official did not turn up, and the pilot said, "Why don't I weigh all of you?" He found that the combined weight of our four children and me would have been no more than that of the official (who was large). So he offered to take us all with Stewart. On the flight, we could see below us the little round tukuls in the various villages and the mountainous terrain. The pilot warned us that to land on the small airstrip on the top of the mountain, he had to aim just below the top, and the air currents would inevitably pull the plane up to land correctly. I was wearing trousers because it was a cold Addis morning. However, in Ethiopian villages trousers are only worn by immoral women; and so when I arrived I was hastily hustled away by the ladies and lent a skirt. The highlight of our two-day visit was walking through the local forest and seeing Geraza monkeys flying from branch to branch in the treetops with their black and white mantle spread out. Stewart was able to teach the physiotherapist how to prevent paralysis in the leprosy patients. Later, the physiotherapist developed amoebic dysentery, which often starts with fairly mild symptoms. She went back for home leave to the USA, but very sadly, we heard that she had died there from a complication of this disease. Presumably, the doctors looking after her were not so familiar with this disease as we were in Ethiopia. Gut diseases, such as amoebic dysentery, were easily acquired by eating uncooked vegetables and salad. In Ethiopia, our family always ate only cooked food.

One day a young Austrian medical student called Gerhard turned up at our house. He had just travelled through Israel and Egypt at the time of the six-day war – quite a feat. He was a determined and persistent person, and wanted to help leprosy patients in Ethiopia. He would appear regularly at our house in the evenings, cold and hungry, because he had no money and had given his only coat to a leprosy beggar. He was musical and would sit down and play our piano while I prepared some food; and Stewart would find a sweater to give him. He would often fall asleep. At one stage he slept in the cemetery with the leprosy patients. We left Ethiopia after two years but Gerhard continued working there. Sadly, we heard a few years later that he had developed hepatitis and died.

In the south east of Ethiopia, near the Ogaden desert, are two towns – Dire Dawa and Harrar. Dire Dawa is on the railway line from Addis to Djibouti by the sea. The Ethiopians who live in this area are a different tribe to the Amharas of Addis Ababa. One school holiday, we booked to stay at the Mennonite Guest House in Dire Dawa, and set off on the 520 km drive there. Halfway, to break the journey, we stayed at a tented Game Park on the Awash River. The owner of the park showed us a tank full of baby crocodiles; the children were fascinated. That evening, we saw oryx, wart hog, kudu, and antelope. We were warned that hippos would lumber out of the river at night to forage on anything left outside the tents, including plastic plates. Fortunately, we spent a peaceful night. It had rained a lot during the night, and the bridges had all been broken several years ago and had not been repaired. I recorded that we drove through forty river beds, "fortunately most of them dry", but a fast-flowing river crossed the road in several places. Whenever the river looked a bit deeper, Stewart would ask me, "Please will you get out and walk through the water to check how deep it is." So obediently I would climb out of the car and paddle across. To our relief, it was never too deep even for our standard car, and the children thought it was great fun to walk through the water, splashing as they went. Stewart had learnt the correct technique to drive through relatively deep water. This involved going into the lowest gear and never taking his foot off the accelerator, to ensure that water wasn't sucked up the exhaust pipe. Some people put a tube from their exhaust onto their roof, but we never did this. Thankfully, we got through all the rivers alright. It had rained heavily, and as this was the main road for heavy lorries, their big wheels had gouged out deep furrows in the mud road. The span of the lorry wheels was larger than our little car, and so Stewart had to drive very carefully. Fortunately, it was downhill. We all found it an alarming journey, and my remark that day has been remembered by all the family: "I will not come back this way!"

However, there was no other road back to Addis, and much to my relief, the road was somewhat better when we returned.

At the Guest House in Dire Dawa, Stewart learnt that there were some ancient caves not far from the town, which was exciting for him, as he is fascinated by all things ancient. Before I knew what was happening, Stewart had asked another visitor, a man with a Land Rover, if he would take us all there, and the Guest House Manager offered to guide us. So the next morning we drove through a dusty valley and passed an isolated hut surrounded by a thick thorn fence, which we were told was to keep out lions. Fortunately, we saw no lions on our trek, probably because it was in the heat of the day. We had to leave the car at a river, where we all waded across. We walked to the base of a steep cliff and had to climb up it, hanging on to trees. With the two other men and Stewart and I, there was one adult to look after each of our four young children. At the top we circumnavigated a large thorny bush via a very narrow ledge with a precipice below us, to reach a tunnel opening. We went in, disturbing some bats, but soon had to turn at a right angle and crouch through a low cross-tunnel passage to a big cave. This is where the paintings were – where people had lived ten thousand years ago with a good view over the countryside. Our guide had brought an old-fashioned spray-gun filled with water. When he sprayed the wall, up came these black, clear ancient painting of animals (made when the valley was lush) – elephants, many kinds of wild animal, and figures of humans and the kind of traps that they used in those days. The paintings were similar to ones in the caves at Lascaux in France, which Stewart saw many years later. The paintings were made out of soot and animal fat, and leapt out in black relief; this caused us all great excitement. Stewart of course took photos of them all and also found a small hand-axe, later confirmed by the British Museum as ten thousand years old.[22] This hand-axe was smaller than the much older one he had found previously. We then had to retrace our steps back through the main cave, through the adjoining tunnel and bats, and out into the exit. There we had to circumnavigate again the large thorny bush, go down the steep cliff, and we trekked back to the car safely.

---

[22] On our return, he gave a set of his photos to the eldest daughter of the Emperor, who then gave a generous gift to the leprosy hospital for Stewart's research. She had never seen these paintings before.

The next day we drove to the nearby town of Harrar. It had a rather unpleasant atmosphere, and we didn't stay long. On the way to Harrar we saw girls of the local tribe – dark-skinned with colourful dresses and interesting hair styles; they were quite different to the women in Addis. In the town we passed wild desert men with large daggers in their belts. Every night the hyenas roamed through the town eating any refuse in the narrow streets, and every evening a man fed hyenas just outside the town. We realised that the hyenas would be more interested in the food that he gave them than in us as

potential meals. So, with some trepidation, we went out to see what was going on. We were amazed to see that the man would hold a piece of meat between his teeth, and the hyenas would lunge up and take it from him. After taking a few photos, we returned to Dire Dawa. Fortunately, our drive back to Addis was uneventful, and we were able to make the whole five hundred kilometres in one day.

On another trip out of Addis, the petrol station we expected was not there. We used the petrol in the spare can and prayed hard, while the petrol gauge stayed firmly at 'Empty'; but we were still able to drive, miraculously. Rounding a corner in a remote hilly area, we saw a young man sitting by the side of the road next to a large drum of petrol. He was smoking a cigarette, and when we drew up he produced a plastic tube, which he put into the drum. He then sucked up the petrol and put the end of the tube into our tank. He continued smoking all the time, and we prayed hard that we would not all end up in a furnace of burning petrol! We drove safely away, thanking God.

The Government restricted the import of any books that they thought might disturb the populace. On one occasion I was sent a recent book written by Dervla Murphy, 'Travels on a donkey in Ethiopia', which described the primitive state of the country where she travelled. I wrote:

Getting it out of customs in the Post Office was quite an adventure. They examined the book suspiciously, looked at all the photos and the titles of the chapters, and then asked me if I had read it! Then they sent me to see the Minister of Information. So, accompanied by a guard, I got into our car and drove with him to the Ministry of Information. With much bowings of the guard, he talked to a man behind a desk, and they completely ignored me. I interrupted and asked for an explanation of what was going on. The official said I could have the book, but first I had to take the guard back to the Post Office. On the way back, the guard asked me for a bribe, which I refused to give him. So, when we got back to the Post Office he tried to make things difficult. Eventually, and much to my relief, I was handed the book and quickly left.

Many of the officials under Haile Selassie were corrupt, and the ordinary people began to be resentful. In early March 1969, I wrote in a letter:

There seems to be trouble in the town today, and all Ethiopian schools have been closed, and also the University. There is talk that the Minister of Defence is under house arrest! Fortunately, it has not been too bad for us, particularly as we live on the edge of the city. People have told us that the feeling is not so anti-foreign this year but is anti-Government and anti-Royal-Family. Bruce has got chickenpox, so he would not have gone to school anyway. The funny part is that we did not realise it was chickenpox to start with and thought it was flea bites; fleas are very common in Ethiopia! We have developed a good way of checking whether any of us have acquired fleas on our body or in our clothes. We stand in the bath and take off our clothes carefully, and shake them. If any fleas are present, they are easily seen against the white of the bath and are immediately squashed. When we did this with Bruce, no fleas appeared, and we realised he must have chickenpox.

In my next letter I wrote:

Ruth remarked tonight at bath time, "Won't it be nice to be back in England without fleas!" Last weekend we had a trip to Sodere with a friend. The sun shone and was hot, and the water was just right, and we all enjoyed it so much. It was good for all Bruce's chickenpox marks too. Our friend had brought some pomegranates and we enjoyed them. It is ages since I have had some and they were very tasty.

We were due to leave Ethiopia in August 1969, and in May Stewart was relieved that an intelligent young Dutch doctor arrived in ALERT to take over much of his work. Later, I wrote:

It is marvellous to have this nice young Dutch doctor here and his wife, who is also a doctor but is expecting their first baby in about a week. He is so interested in the work and in leprosy neuritis and eyes – a man after Stewart's heart! He is learning quickly, and he is taking over Stewart's work in the hospital and in the clinics, just keeping a few of the problem cases for Stewart to see. Now I hope Stewart will have more time for all the medical papers that he has been trying to write and for his laboratory work too, instead of trying to write papers in the evening when he is weary.

After two years, it was time to leave. Stewart was actually replaced by three doctors to do his work. August 8th was the date for our departure.

I look back on our momentous days in this ancient country and realise I have not mentioned many other remarkable experiences we had there. Five years after we left Addis, there was a series of violent coups against the Emperor and his Government, which led finally to the rule of the most murderous man – the Communist, Mengistu Haile Mariam. The Emperor was smothered in his bed, and his daughters, granddaughters and family were imprisoned for fourteen years. To subdue the population, his troops murdered one boy in every family suspected of being opposed to his rule. He also forbade the movement of food from the south of the country to the north, which played a large part in the development of the terrible famine in 1983.

CHAPTER SEVEN

1969 – in England for seven years; and joining Stewart when he lectured in Australia.

Leaving Ethiopia

We wanted to find an interesting way to travel back to England rather than just a direct flight. So Stewart asked The Leprosy Mission to give us the money for our air tickets and we would arrange our own journey. We had found that for the same amount of money, all six of us could fly to Athens, stay two nights there, then take a boat to Venice, stay two nights there, on by train to Paris for two nights, and then hop across the Channel by air to Southampton – where Stewart's parents would meet us. A French travel agent in Addis made the bookings.

The Suez Canal was still closed, due to the war going on between Israel and Egypt. Luggage by sea from Ethiopia had to go round Africa to England, which would take at least six weeks. So we had to take with us, in our suitcases, sheets and everything we would need until our luggage arrived. It came to thirteen suitcases in all, but very fortunately the airline did not charge us for the extra luggage! Actually, our trunks did not arrive in England until the beginning of December due to a fire on the ship, and our sheets and pillows all smelled of smoke.

Flying from Addis to Athens took us down the length of the Nile River, and it was amazing to see from the air how narrow the strip of houses and fields was, with the desert stretched away on either side. Arriving at Athens, we were shocked to hear that there had just been a bomb explosion in the airport, which had killed an English tourist.

We went in two taxis to our hotel, but when we got there – being cautious as always after our worldwide travels – Stewart got out alone and was horrified when the receptionist said, "Oh! So sorry – you are booked tomorrow. I have no empty rooms tonight!"

He asked her, "Can you recommend any other hotel?" This was rather optimistic, as of course in Athens in August all hotel rooms would be booked.

The receptionist replied, "I have just seen a large coach departing from a hotel up the road. Perhaps you could go and inquire there."

We were glad we had not yet got out of our two taxis, and we prayed hard. Amazingly, when we got to the next hotel, the receptionist told Stewart, "Yes, we have a lot of empty rooms; they have just been vacated! I have a double room for you and your wife, with an adjoining door to a bedroom with four beds." That was a real provision by God for the six of us.

Our memories of Athens include eating enormous ripe, juicy peaches that we bought cheaply in the market. We were fortunate that in 1969, the Acropolis and the Parthenon were open to visitors, and we had a wonderful walk there in the afternoon sunshine. A photo of Caroline, taken on an ancient stone pillar, is one she treasures. We enjoyed swimming at Glyfada beach.

We then caught a Zim-line (Jewish) boat from the nearby port of Piraeus, and found that we were the only Gentiles among six hundred Jews from many countries in Europe on the boat. They had been visiting Israel and were happily returning to their countries. They treated us well and approved of our eldest daughter being called Ruth (which she also found useful when she lived on a kibbutz in Israel many years later). Our route to Venice took us through the very narrow Corinth Canal. Not long before, there had been a bomb explosion in a Zim-line travel office in London. So, being a Zim-line boat, when we went through the Corinth Canal, the Jewish officers on board lined the deck with guns on their hips, in case somebody tried to drop a bomb onto our boat from one of the frequent bridges across the canal. As Gentiles, we had to learn how to have our coffee after meals without milk – the kosher way.

The boat sailed into Venice as dawn was breaking, and our first sight of that incredible city was the Plaza of San Marco appearing through the mist in the early morning – an unforgettable sight. So there we were in Venice with four young children between the ages of four and nine, and thirteen suitcases! We planned to deposit our excess suitcases at the train terminal left-luggage department. However, when we got to Venice Station by water-bus – counting our suitcases on and off the bus – we found a huge queue, because a bomb had gone off in the station the day before. Not another one! We realised we could not wait for hours in the station, so we went back to the water-bus with all our suitcases and then to a hotel on the beautiful Ponte Rialto, where we were booked for two nights. We had a marvellous time in Venice looking at the wonderful canals and St Mark's Cathedral – golden in the afternoon sun – and all the fantastic things to see there.

We then caught the train from Venice to Paris, enjoying the countryside and the scenic snow-covered mountains of Switzerland. We saw clear mountain streams, grassy meadows and wooden chalets; and the children rushed from side to side of the train to see all they could. When we got to Paris – at ten o'clock at night – we were due to be met by the Thomas Cook agent, who knew our hotel and would take us to it. However, arriving at Paris there was no agent to meet us on the platform! We prayed hard (again!) and Stewart went off to a little kiosk in the centre of the station that arranged hotels for visitors. Once again, because it was August in Paris, one would expect all the hotels to be full. However, the receptionist there said, "I have a new hotel that has just opened; a very small one. I think it has only four beds vacant, but you're welcome to try it." She phoned, and they were happy to have us – another miracle. So off we went, and we were able to put two children in each bed – head to toe.

We enjoyed 'chocolat et croissants' for breakfast the next morning in the vine-covered courtyard. We went to see the Mona Lisa, the Eiffel Tower and other sights in Paris. The following morning we took two taxis to the airport. For some reason which we forget, the woman driver of one of the two taxis took umbrage at something Stewart said. She stopped the taxi, jumped out and said she was not going to take us to the airport. We had to explain that we meant no offence and would give her a little bit more money (perhaps that's what she wanted all the time), and we finally got to the airport only a short time before the flight was due out. There was nobody else waiting at the reception desk, and so we checked in everything very quickly and walked rapidly to the steps of the small aircraft flying to Southampton. I went up the steps to see where we could sit and found that there were only six isolated seats all round the small plane; fortunately our four children were well cared for by their neighbours during the flight. So it was that we arrived in Southampton, and there were Stewart's parents waiting to greet us. They kindly drove us back to our home in Fareham, Hampshire, where we had been living before we went to Ethiopia.

This was English life again. Stewart returned to his job in the Portsmouth Laboratory, and we settled into our house in Fareham. Bruce went to nursery school; Ruth, Caroline and Timothy to primary school in Fareham; and we acquired a cat. However, our children did take time to adjust into English school ways, after having studied in American schools. It was a pleasure to worship again at St John's Church in Fareham, with its active Sunday school for children. With the encouragement of the minister, Stewart applied to become an Anglican lay reader[23] in the Diocese of Portsmouth. The Bishop agreed and licensed Stewart to work in the parish of St John's, Fareham, and in other Anglican churches in the area – when the resident minister was away or sick. We continued to enjoy going to Lee-on-Solent in the summer – and in the winter with crashing waves on the shore. The ideal country walks in the wonderful woods were just a short drive inland. Bruce, at the age of five, kept up well with his elder brother and sisters.

Soon after we arrived back, there was a local outbreak of acute meningitis in the Portsmouth area, and Stewart was busy helping to control this. The Laboratory also included the brucellosis reference laboratory for the United Kingdom. He wished to take a higher degree in Pathology and Microbiology, which would allow him to apply for a Consultant Microbiologist post in a hospital. So he worked hard and passed the 'Membership' of the Royal College of Pathologists of England (only a third of candidates passed). The written exam included questions on brucellosis and meningitis, and the Director of the Portsmouth Laboratory said to Stewart, "This paper was obviously devised for you by 'Someone up there'!"

---

[23] non-ordained assistant minister

A Christian friend of Stewart's was now a Consultant in Infectious Diseases at a new hospital in Northwick Park, near Harrow, north-west London. He suggested that Stewart should apply for the (Second) Consultant Microbiologist post at Northwick Park. The interview for the post was in February 1971, and Stewart was appointed. So we began house-hunting in that area and especially in Northwood, two or three miles from Harrow. We found only one or two houses that might suit us. Then a friend of ours teaching in a Northwood Girls School mentioned our need of a home to a couple who were selling their six-bedroom house in Northwood. After we visited them, they agreed to sell us their house in preference to other buyers. The house was in a quiet area, with a bedroom for each of our children, a spare room and a large garden. We managed to raise the mortgage to buy it, based on the sale of our house in Fareham, although selling that proved difficult.

Outside our Northwood home

We moved to Northwood in June. Ruth and Caroline enjoyed the Girls' Grammar School in Northwood Hills, while Tim went to the local boys' fee-paying junior school – St Martin's School – just down the road from our new house. Bruce had to go to the local state primary school for a term, but there were no organised games there and he had little outlet for all his energy. In September he joined Tim at St Martin's, and he and Tim particularly enjoyed the excellent facilities for games there.

Many visitors stayed with us, including Stewart's parents, other relatives and friends, and an exchange student from France with Ruth. Soon after arriving in Northwood, I acquired a miniature dachshund called Flippy, who would follow me anywhere. There was a fine Anglican Church in Northwood, and the vicar welcomed Stewart as a lay reader. The church had many Christian activities for children and teenagers, and organised extensive visiting in houses in the neighbourhood. Our children enjoyed the local 'Crusader' (Christian) meetings for young people on Sunday afternoons; and on Thursday evenings, we had a Bible study group for adults in our home. Several church people became good friends.

For our summer holidays, we went to Abersoch in North Wales, which had wide beaches and Christian seaside activities for young people in the holidays. We went there every year for four years, hiring a caravan in a beach caravan park in the sand dunes, a walk of only a minute or two from the beach. We enjoyed the drive there through the Welsh hills, especially as we went near the village where, in 1800, a young Welsh girl, Mary Jones, had walked barefoot for fourteen miles in an effort to buy a Bible. This resulted in the formation of the Bible Society, which has provided Bibles for many language groups around the world ever since. 'Mary Jones' had been one of the many stories that we had read over the years to our children, including during mealtimes.

One year we wanted to climb Snowdon, hopefully going part of the way up on the special little train. However, when we got there the train booking was full. So we decided to walk to the first station, but again there were no tickets, and so we all walked to the top, relying on our little dachshund to faithfully follow me. At the top, mist covered the summit. We opened the door of the refreshment café, and one man called out, "Was that an Alsatian when you started at the bottom?" Flippy had very sore little legs for several days after that marathon walk. Perhaps he is the only dachshund to have ever climbed all the way to the top of Snowdon.

There was a large local swimming pool in Northwood Hills, and for the birthdays of our two sons, we initiated a 'swimming breakfast'. Rather bemused parents would bring their boys at 8:00 a.m. on a Saturday; then, in our car (not subject to seatbelt rules in those days), we took the boys to the swimming pool. They would get rid of a lot of energy and come back for breakfast in our house. Quite extensive woods were not far from where we lived, where we enjoyed walking. On other birthdays, Stewart laid a trail of flour through the woods for the boys to follow and exhaust their energy before we had a birthday tea.

Our four lovely children were all growing rapidly, with increasing needs for warm clothes and shoes, which they grew out of remarkably quickly! With high inflation in those days, the cost of food, heating, the house mortgage, and the local authority tax increased steadily, while Stewart's salary after tax stayed almost the same. Our years on a minimal salary were catching up with us. We had not built up a cash reserve enabling us to buy our house without a mortgage (as most of Stewart's contemporaries had done before their families grew up). I decided to do a refresher course in nursing, but it was difficult to get family-friendly times of work. Reluctantly, I stopped this work after six months.

One day, after returning from shopping, I heard our little dog barking furiously (which was unusual) and found him shut behind the drawing-room door, where I never left him. Very sadly, I discovered that our most valuable wedding presents had been stolen, including a rare tea set from old China. Also, my dressing table had been ransacked and all my precious jewels removed. I rang the police, and they discovered that a downstairs window had been forced. They gave us no hope that the items would ever be found. We immediately installed a burglar alarm, but it was a case of 'locking the stable door after the horse has got out'.

My father died when he was eighty-four. In the front of his well-marked Bible, my mother wrote, "Pat has gone to glory – May 1973." This Bible is one of my treasures. Many tributes were paid to him for his role as Headmaster of Chefoo School in North China with the arduous task of looking after the schoolchildren in prison camp for several years and then bringing them all out safely. My dear mother was desolate after Dad died, and she lived only another six months. She came from such a different generation to mine and had been brought up in the far west of China. I felt I never knew her very well. While we were in China she had been a busy headmaster's wife and I was the youngest child; then, in prison camp, I was not living in the same room as them but with other girls in my dormitory; and when we came to England I was at boarding school and then worked away from home.

Stewart's parents lived on the South Coast. They enjoyed coming and staying with us and seeing our family grow up. However, the car journey to the South Coast from Northwood took a long time – not easy for our four young children. We did it on occasions when Stewart could get time off.

In addition to his hospital and laboratory duties, Stewart did research into new antibiotics, including their absorption in human volunteers. In early 1973, a letter landed on Stewart's desk inviting him to give the first 'Annual Glaxo Oration' in Melbourne in June that year and then lecture for a month in every state of Australia. This was followed by a phone call from Sir Robert Noad, President of the Australian Medical Association. "This is Bob Noad. We do hope you will be our Glaxo Orator and then lecture on your antibiotic research. Please send me titles of any other subjects that you think our doctors might like to hear about." For his Oration, Stewart chose the title, 'Newer aspects of Antibiotic Therapy in Developed and Developing Countries', and prepared lectures on different aspects of antibiotic treatment and on leprosy.

When Stewart flew off to Australia, he carefully kept his lecture slides with him on board the plane. When he arrived in Melbourne, he was told, "The last lecturer here [the President of the Royal College of Physicians] put his slides in his luggage and they were delivered to Japan!" Stewart delivered the Oration in his scarlet Cambridge MD robes, after which he was presented with a silver salver. He included a few slides of Ethiopia where the ratio of doctors to patients is among the lowest in the world. He mentioned ancient Egyptian medicine and also gently suggested to his audience that the welfare of Australia might depend on them "taking the pulse of Asian countries", as Australia weaned itself from other English-speaking countries, all rather far away.

He then lectured in every state, often advising on the best antibiotic combination to treat patients with the worst infections. A few years later in Sydney, he found they were still following his advice. On the other side of the country, in Perth, he was asked to lecture twice on leprosy. Sixty years earlier, the north of Western Australia had had an influx of Chinese fishermen who had brought leprosy with them, which then spread among the Australian Aborigine population. In Perth, John, a local microbiologist, helped him to hire a small plane cheaply for a day, which took them to the unique Karri-tree forests in the south of the State. These trees are so hard that one across a river can easily take the weight of a lorry; and they drove over 'One Tree Bridge'. On the way home in the plane, John said, "I've never seen my State from the air before!"

My twin aunts, when they heard that Stewart was going to Australia, very kindly offered to pay my air-fare, so that I could join him during his last week in that country. We planned to meet in Alice Springs, so I flew there via Darwin, changing planes in Singapore. However, when I landed at 2:00 a.m. at Darwin airport, the officials treated me as a suspect person – possibly because my passport said, "Born in China", and at that time Australia was very wary of Communist China. Every single thing was taken out of my suitcase, and the case itself was examined for concealed compartments! Nothing suspicious was found, but they did apologise saying, "Sorry, Madam!" and bundled everything back into my suitcase. Not the best experience at that time in the morning and after a long flight.

In Alice Springs, Stewart met me, and we enjoyed the rugged scenery near the town. We then flew to Queensland and had a wonderful weekend in Cairns, exploring the Barrier Reef and driving into the Atherton Tableland forest. We flew back to England via Hong Kong and went to the Leprosy Island, meeting blind Mr Wong[24]. From Hong Kong we went to the Seychelles Islands where we knew an English couple who were helping to build a big Christian radio station. They gave us a great welcome, and the Seychelles beaches were a treasure trove for shells. We also saw one of the last amazing giant Seychelles tortoises.

Later, in the school summer holidays, Stewart was due to lecture at the Centennial International Leprosy Congress in Bergen, Norway. Leprosy bacteria had first been described by the physician Hansen[25] in 1873 in Bergen. As Stewart had been given the money to travel

---

[24] See chapter 4 for a description of Mr Wong
[25] In the USA, leprosy is called 'Hansen's disease'

there, we decided to use that towards a holiday in Norway. So all six of us and our car went by sea from Newcastle to Bergen, and after the Congress, we travelled round the country for two weeks, staying economically in youth hostels. We reached Trondheim in the north, and I wrote to friends:

> *Some roads seem worse than in Ethiopia! – steep, winding, and very narrow with loose gravel on the surface, and deep pot-holes. However, the lasting impression was of beautiful scenery, with many fjords, peaks covered in snow, waterfalls and two pale-blue glaciers with water the colour of jade running out from below the ice.*

In November 1974, Stewart's mother had a severe heart attack and probably only survived because his doctor father looked after her in their home in Sussex. Stewart rushed down to see her and then visited her for one day every month. Ruth became a member of a fine youth choir, 'Jesus Is', which sang all over the country. Caroline was doing well at Northwood Hills School and was acquiring a wide general knowledge from her extensive reading. Timothy had won the tennis cup, and Bruce was captain of soccer 'Colts' and had his cricket and rugby colours. Every night, Stewart read the Bible and prayed with each of them.

However, by January next year, we were having great difficulty in balancing our monthly budget, and we had an increasing bank overdraft. In the UK, inflation had been rising steadily, and by 1975 it reached 22%! Stewart's salary did not keep pace with this, and so no wonder we were having great difficulty feeding and clothing our growing family. Finally, we saw no alternative but to sell our house, move into a smaller one to reduce or eliminate our mortgage, and move Tim and Bruce from the fee-paying St Martin's School to the state system. Bruce would have to go back to the nearby state primary school for a year, where he had been most unhappy, particularly as there were no organised games. Tim was now too old to take the '11-plus' examination for entrance to the local grammar school. He would have to move to the local 'secondary modern' school, which was not of a high academic standard. This would seriously limit his chance of university education.

In his medical journals, Stewart began to notice advertisements for Microbiologist jobs in Australia. In his diary on January 6, 1975 Stewart wrote:

Shall we consider going to Australia? Discussed the possibility with our children.

We would never have considered going to live there, if Stewart and I had not had the opportunity to see the country two years earlier.

In March, he saw an advertisement for a combined academic/hospital Microbiology post in Perth, Western Australia (WA). As he had achieved a Cambridge Doctorate, he was eligible for the academic post, although he had not yet worked in a university position. We recognised that it might be an answer to our financial problems, and we constantly prayed about the whole situation.

A major consideration was that Stewart's parents were getting older. His father was very fit and able to look after his mother, who had partially recovered but was now very dependent. We realised that if we were in Australia and some prolonged crisis in his father's health demanded our return, we would do this. However, as we prayed, we did not have any sense that this needed to sway our decision. Air travel was becoming much easier, and as Stewart attended medical conferences around the world at least once a year, he would make sure he included a visit to his parents. In the event, Stewart's mother died suddenly in November 1984, and Stewart's father remained physically fit, living in their house until his very sudden death six months later.[26]

Stewart wrote to Perth to find out more about the appointment; and in early May, the Head of the WA University Microbiology Department flew to London to see Stewart and asked him to apply for the post. Stewart flew to Perth in September for the interview and to see all aspects of the post and possible schools for the family. He was glad to meet an old Chefoo friend, Alf Binks, now an accountant in Perth, and they concluded that Stewart's university salary would be adequate for our needs. In October, Stewart received a letter offering him the post of Reader (Associate Professor) in Clinical Microbiology

---

[26] It turned out that our children also visited them, and when Caroline lived in England she often stayed with them.

in the Microbiology Department of the University of Western Australia, and Head of the Department of Microbiology at the Royal Perth Hospital (RPH).

So after more prayer and much discussion with our family, we felt it was the right move to go to Perth, even though it was a momentous decision to make. As I had parents and grandparents who had travelled to and from China, and thousands of miles inside China often in difficult circumstances, I was never too troubled at changing continents. With Stewart, I had lived in India and Hong Kong, then back in England, and then to Ethiopia and back. But it was going to be very difficult for our children, who in their young lives had experienced changing schools quite often, losing friends and adapting to new places and new customs.

In view of the fact that we were selling our house and moving to Australia, our bank manager agreed to us increasing our overdraft. So we took the opportunity for all of us to see more of our own country and Europe before flying off to the Southern Hemisphere. In the April holidays, we went to Jersey for a few days. Stewart, with his interest in archaeology, knew of the ancient megalithic stone structure of Hogue Bie. Its corridor and roof of huge stones was dramatic. Caroline still remembers it vividly. In the early summer holidays, we were lent a holiday apartment in the coastal resort of Estartit, in northern Spain. We piled into our car, drove through France, and found our way there. We loved swimming and sunbathing, and visited Barcelona, where we walked up the Ramblas past numerous tubs of wonderful, colourful flowers and took the cable car to the monastery of Montserrat, with its famous 'Black Virgin' statue. For our return trip, we drove across Spain to Santander and caught the ferry to Southampton – and so back home. During the last week of August, we enjoyed a few days in Gairloch on the West Coast of Scotland.

We put our house in Northwood on the market but only managed to get a low price, due to the poor economic state of the country and the housing market at that time. We wrote to our relatives and friends, explaining the background to our decision to go to Australia, and concluded:

> *Provided the necessary visas are granted we hope to leave for*
> *Perth in January, so that the children can start the new*

Australian school year in February. It is likely to be very hot then, but we are looking forward to the sunshine. Of course we are all very sorry to leave our native land, our friends, our neighbourhood and the hospital – all that we have come to know and appreciate. We ask you to pray for each of us, and particularly for our children, that we may settle in Perth and make good Christian friends there.

On January 8th, 1976 we flew to Australia, with a stop in Cairo to see the pyramids and a camel ride in the shadow of these amazing structures. We found Cairo to be a busy, crowded, noisy city but enjoyed the Museum and saw the golden mask of Tutankhamen.

At breakfast in our hotel we were offered orange juice to drink. Stewart asked the man, "Please may I see it."

He brought a bucket of orange-coloured liquid and Stewart asked, "What is the orange juice diluted in?"

He replied, "Neeley water," which we realised meant "Nile water" – obviously very contaminated!

We declined his offer, and stayed free from stomach problems. We travelled on to Singapore and visited the Botanical Gardens with their beautiful orchids; then finally on to Perth, Western Australia.

CHAPTER EIGHT

1976 – Perth, Australia for fourteen years; worldwide lecture travels together.

*J*anuary is the middle of summer 'Down Under', and it was wonderfully hot in Perth when we arrived – a dry heat, not the humidity that we found so difficult in Hong Kong. One of our first outings was, naturally, to the beach. Big waves were rolling in, so we were cautious – but not so a large man, who was knocked over and apparently unconscious, rolling in the surf. Stewart pulled him up from the waves and he recovered, but his first remark was, "I've got sand in my bathers[27]." He didn't seem particularly grateful or surprised at his situation! It only took ten minutes by car to reach the sea from our home, and the hot weather in Perth (30-44°C between November and March) was conducive to swimming. We have happy memories of the beaches that extend for many miles up and down the coast. It rarely rained between October and May, and in the wet season often rained only at night. The winter temperature was almost never below 13°C. Tennis could be played on virtually every day of the year, and we joined the local tennis club that had grass courts. Tim and Bruce are skilful tennis players and were regularly the top junior pair of our local tennis club, which usually won the interclub competition.

Stewart started his work in Royal Perth Hospital and the University of Western Australia (WA), and a university house was provided for us, after two weeks in a local hotel. Everybody was helpful, and one of the microbiology doctors kindly lent us her car

---

[27] swimming trunks

until we were able to buy one. We found an older bungalow near the university that we could just afford, but it needed an extension and modernisation. The kitchen cooking stove was fuelled solely by logs of wood; but it had a lovely shaded front verandah and was just a short bicycle ride from the university. In nearly all the residential areas of Perth the houses were bungalows with a lawn front and back. A mild-natured Australian architect was recommended to us, but his workman was a red-headed Irishman, and one day I came home to find them up on the roof arguing. The Irishman was threatening to throw the architect from the roof onto the ground. Action was needed urgently! I promptly ordered them both down – I wouldn't tolerate such behaviour on my property. Fortunately, reason prevailed and they both came calmly down, as I wished.

Our belongings eventually arrived in Perth in June, but missing one precious small box of Stewart's, in which he had some of his most prized letters. Such is the travail of travelling around the world. So we moved into our house in the suburb of Nedlands in July 1976 and were pleased to have our own place. Late in the year, I wrote a long letter to my friends and relatives back in England:

> Here are a few of our first impressions of this land of great distances. To travel just a few miles out of Perth is to be in flat bush country, sometimes fascinating and sometimes dull. Just behind Perth are the Darling Ranges, with beautiful wooded country. Everywhere, undesirable insects seem to abound, though fortunately we have not met many. Perth is built on sand, and sand seems to be everywhere, penetrating into cars and carpets, washing machines and hoovers. Our garden required a lot of work. It was just a sand patch, and so Stewart planted individual pieces of tough grass and put in a framework of pipes and sprinklers. We now have a complete lawn, impervious to the hottest sun as long as we can go on watering it. We have planted various fruit trees and have some lovely roses in the front garden.
>
> Western Australia has beautiful wildflowers, which are seen at their best in the spring here – October and November – many varieties and some so very small. Wild white freesias with a beautiful scent abound in the huge 'King's Park' in the middle of Perth. We have not had good rains this year, and the reservoirs are much down on their usual level. Resulting water restrictions

mean we cannot water our lawn from the main supply, but we have been fortunate to share the cost of a well with a neighbour, who happens to run a company making such wells!

I have been doing some work for Stewart at hospital recently, and one of the fascinating things has been the names of the different people who have come to live in WA: Italian, Russian, Latvian, Czech, Greek, Armenian and many more. If one of these people comes to my door, I might recognise their origin by their colouring or the cast of their features, but as soon as they speak, they are obviously Australian – the younger generation. Many men wear shorts and long socks, even to work, and in the shops it is difficult for men to buy anything but white or blue shirts.

Last night we went to hear the 'Messiah' at the Perth Concert Hall and much enjoyed it. There is also a huge Entertainment Centre, where we watched tennis. We have seen the Harlem Globe-Trotters, the Ballet Carmen and Siberian Cossack Dancers, which were excellent. Stewart and I are both on the committee for the Christian Foundation for the Blind. They look forward to a yearly function just before Christmas, and we are helping.

It has taken time to settle into Australia. Our family have left their school and church friends behind in England, so Perth is a particularly hard adjustment for them. Ruth and Caroline are at the local grammar school. Tim started in the first year of the senior school of Scotch College, while Bruce has had to spend one year at the junior school. Bruce reacted forcefully to an Aussie boy who called him a 'Pommy bastard'. He gave the boy a hard punch on the chin, which knocked him down. Bruce was called 'Bruiser' after that, and no one has called him a Pom again! Because Ruth's birthday is in December, she is pleased that she can go to the University of Western Australia in 1977. Caroline is maturing into such a nice person to have around. Stewart enjoys swimming, and tennis with Tim and Bruce.

We have come to rely on each other in the family much more, and have long and interesting discussions around the supper table, with everyone contributing. We regularly have people to Sunday lunch and on other occasions. Although we live on a tight budget, good food including meat is much cheaper than it was in England. I have to provide meals for six hungry people

*every day. With the hot weather, clothes dry quickly; but there is
a lot for me to do.*

*I have not mentioned the Aboriginal people of Australia[28]. They
are unlike any other race that we have met in the world. It is sad
that they seem unable to cope with city life, where they have
many problems with alcohol. They are superb in their own
environment, tracking and living in the inhospitable desert areas
of Australia and finding their way in the bush. We recently
entertained a couple of Australians who have taken the Christian
Gospel to the heart of the country, in the desert eight hundred
miles west of Alice Springs. It was fascinating to learn some of
the customs of the Aborigines who have lived in this land for
fifty thousand years.*

The city overlooking Perth Water

When we arrived in Perth, it was still a relatively small city, easy
to get around. For me, however, England was still home, and I never
really fitted into Australia. I felt very English, and I'm sure in some
ways this was a bit of a barrier. It took time to make friends; but it
wasn't long before we acquired an adorable little puppy – a Golden
Retriever. 'Casper' rapidly became a wonderful part of our family
and was with us for thirteen years – much loved and enjoyed. Our
home was near the large salt-water Perth Water, which was three
miles inland from where the narrow Swan River reached the sea.
Casper and I had many a happy walk there, and he always dived into
the clear water on hot summer days.

---

[28] First Australians

Our first Christmas Day in Australia found us on the large 'Leighton' beach, fifteen minutes' drive from our home, swimming, sunbathing and playing beach cricket. I made a full Christmas dinner for the evening. This was our pattern every year, and our visitors for dinner included African students who had escaped from their countries and English students away from home. Whenever any young English person turned up at our church or a member of our family met them, I invited them to our home – initially for Sunday lunch, but if Wimbledon Tennis was on the TV, or there was a cricket test match, they would watch it at our home. Many have remained good family friends.

The school and university holidays in January gave us the opportunity to drive south to the cooler climate at the southwest tip

of Australia – a meeting of two oceans – renting a wooden holiday cottage in the small town of Augusta. Facing east is the Indian Ocean with a rugged rocky coastline, while facing south is the Antarctic Ocean but with huge sandy beaches. We visited the lighthouse at the extreme tip, Cape Leuwin, had picnics on the rocks on the western side where we could see manta rays in the sea below us, and swam and walked on the extensive beaches on the south-facing coast. Augusta became one of my favourite places.

In the May holidays, when it was getting (relatively) cooler in Perth, we drove north to the beautiful resort of Kalbarri. It is situated on a lagoon with a rocky bar out to sea, so that sailing in the lagoon is safe. There are extensive beaches with rocks for climbing, and on one unforgettable occasion we watched a huge wall of surf in which five dolphins were outlined in the wave against the setting sun.

Dolphins enjoy surfing too! One year, from there we drove farther north to Shark Bay and Monkey Mia where dolphins come into the shore and can actually be stroked – an unreal experience. As a family, we also visited the Nambung 'Pinnacles' two hundred miles north of Perth. These amazing natural limestone structures, some as high as sixteen feet, were formed about 27,000 years ago, after the sea receded and left deposits of sea shells. Since then, coastal winds have removed the surrounding sand, leaving the pillars exposed to the elements.

In Australia, joining a church was very important to us. Because there was no evangelical (Bible-believing) Anglican church in Perth at that time, we attended a Baptist church in the north of Perth, to which we were introduced by our good friend from Chefoo days, Alf Binks. We made several friends there. After two years we were glad to hear that David, a young, evangelical Anglican minister, was about to take over St Matthew's church, near our home. On the first Sunday that David was there, Stewart and I were overseas at a medical conference, but our family went there, riding on their bicycles to the church. We worshipped there throughout the rest of our time in Perth. Stewart became the senior pastoral assistant[29]. I was also licensed by the Archbishop of Perth to be a pastoral assistant, and it was a great joy to visit the housebound and take Holy Communion to them. We enjoyed a wide circle of friends in the church, and the church secretary became a particularly good friend. We had a Bible study in our home on Wednesdays to which a variety of people came, including an Afghani Muslim man who asked profound questions and said he loved the Lord Jesus.

Perth is one of the most isolated major cities in the world, and while air travel was relatively cheap, overseas travel from Perth was common. I wrote in March 1979:

Ruth has just arrived back after three months in the British Isles during the University summer holidays. She went to Northern Ireland to visit my cousins there for three weeks and safely drove

---

[29] lay reader

through the border town of Crossmaglen – IRA country – to Dublin! Caroline is now in England, having left in early February. She is due back after Easter, when she will start her nursing studies at Sir Charles Gairdener Hospital, having achieved the high grades in her final school exams required for entry into the Nursing School. Both Ruth and Caroline worked to earn their living expenses in England.

January is our holiday month, but Stewart was on duty in hospital. So we spent our holiday money on a simple 'above-ground' swimming pool. We all have greatly enjoyed this, both for exercise and to cool off. On the day that we all helped fill in the area around the pool with wood chips onto the sand, the temperature was 42.6°C (109°F). The wooden shovel handle was too hot to hold with bare hands!

Stewart was very busy – overseeing his large microbiology laboratory, treating patients with infections in the wards, seeing 'problem' patients referred to him by family doctors (trying new treatments), and doing research on antibiotics. The Deputy Head of the Microbiology Department was John, the Christian doctor whom he had met during his short visit in 1973, who became a good friend. Stewart's Infection Control policy and nurses kept MRSA bacteria from causing infections in the Royal Perth Hospital and throughout WA. MRSA was rife in the other States of Australia. He also organised the Microbiology course for the medical students and taught them on two afternoons each week. He worked a long day but was always home for supper with the family. His evenings seemed too occupied with reading and writing research papers; but when he went to Sydney for a medical conference he took Caroline, and Tim went with him to Melbourne. When Bruce's godfather visited us, Bruce and Stewart took him camping in the forest in the southwest of WA.

Stewart had a university appointment and so, although his salary was lower than that of hospital doctors, he could take six-month Sabbatical (study) leave every three years – most of the time overseas. In December 1979, Stewart took his first such leave – in the UK. He started in the long Australian summer holidays of December to February, so that Tim and Bruce could come with us. Stewart lectured on the way in Japan at Hiroshima, and this was an opportunity for him to face the fact that the Japanese had been his captors while he was their prisoner in China during the war.

Tim, Bruce and I travelled to England on a Qantas plane, but near the end of our long flight, smoke suddenly started to fill the cabin! The oxygen masks came down, and we were told to remain in our seats and stay calm. It was quite frightening, and our prayers went up immediately. We made a very rapid descent into Heathrow but had a safe landing at a remote runway, away from the main area in case our plane burst into flames! All the emergency doors were immediately opened, and it was not long before a burly British policeman appeared saying, "Are you all right down at the back there?" Months later, back in Australia, we had a nice letter from Qantas, apologising and explaining that an electrical fault had caused the smoke.

Those were the days when it was 'fun to fly' – unless there was an emergency. We had plenty of space to sit comfortably in the seats and plenty of space to walk up the wide aisles. It was all so different to economy flights and time-consuming security procedures that we experienced twenty years later.

At this time, I was working as a nurse for a Dermatologist. Three of us worked for him, and I was fortunate that he gave me time off to travel with Stewart when he went overseas to his medical conferences. I really appreciated being able to visit many different continents and countries.

From the south to the north of Western Australia is three thousand miles, and it has a long coastline. The most northerly town of Derby is four hours' flying time from Perth. When Stewart lectured on antibiotics there and in other cities north of Perth, I accompanied him. In Derby, we visited the leprosy hospital nearby. We then flew a short way south to the beautiful little port of Broome, which has a famous 'Eighty Mile Beach'.

On another journey, this time by car, we went to the port of Exmouth, driving for miles and miles on a straight, dusty, empty road with minimal vegetation and the odd dead animal. For a hundred and fifty kilometres we did not pass a single car.

A Christian Sailing Camp at Busselton, 120 miles south of Perth, was an opportunity for Tim and Bruce to learn to sail, and Stewart led the Bible studies for all the teenagers. When our family were in their teens they worked in a summer Christian beach mission in Albany on the south coast of WA, and enjoyed being with other Christian young people, teaching children about Jesus. Farther along the south coast was the town of Esperance, where we went once for a holiday with Tim and Bruce. From there, we drove inland to Kalgoorlie with its gold-mines; they are now abandoned, but there was a gold-rush there in 1900. The streets had been built wide enough to allow camel trains to turn in the road. Of course we went down the one gold-mine open for visitors. WA is very rich in many types of minerals, including some of the biggest iron mines in the world. Just north of Perth is a National Park, with kangaroos, wallabies and koalas bears. It is a lovely place for a day out and picnic with family and friends. We celebrated Caroline's eighteenth birthday there.

The years passed by. Ruth became President of the Christian Union in the University of Western Australia – the first girl to be so. She did a fourth year Honours degree, working in the far north of WA, studying the economic geography of the region and meeting the First Australians (Aborigines) there. Stewart went up to visit her and they swam off a ferry in the middle of huge Lake Argyle, to avoid the crocodiles around the edge! She then won a Rotary scholarship to go to the University of Madras (Chennai) for a year.

Caroline was very pleased to achieve her Nursing Finals at Sir Charles Gairdener Hospital without her tutors realising that her father was Head of Microbiology at Royal Perth Hospital! I wrote to friends:

> *Caroline is back on the wards again after an intrepid holiday travelling by bus and staying in youth hostels on her own all round Australia, often sleeping on the bus seat wrapped in a blanket! She first went across the vast Nullarbor Desert to Adelaide (1600 miles) and then by train up to Alice Springs; on to remote Mount Isa in the outback of Queensland; then to Cairns in the far north of Queensland; down to Brisbane, Sydney, Canberra, Adelaide; and back to Perth. A round-trip of eight thousand miles!*

> *Tim, in his final year at Scotch College, was chosen by the Headmaster to be School Captain. He is also captain of tennis and has beaten the state under-17 champion. He will go on to the University of WA and study English.[30] As I write, Bruce is on a four-day hike with five school friends through bush country*

---

[30] He became President of the Christian Union.

south of Perth, carrying his food and tent with him. Bruce plays chess for the school and usually manages to come away with a trophy of some sort. He will become captain of tennis next year; and the tennis master said to me, "I have never had two brothers following each other as captain of tennis!"

Our family all became very resourceful and independent, perhaps as a consequence of growing up in WA.

The whole family in Australia

In January 1982, during the Australian summer holidays, Stewart had a conference in Canberra, and he decided to drive with Bruce, first to Melbourne and Sydney (2,511 miles[31]) and then back from Canberra, camping all the way. They filled the back of the car with tents, food and drinking water, and I waved them away on a Friday afternoon. Their first stop was in the tiny community of Balladonia, where the first 'Sputnik-Skylab' had fallen to Earth in 1979, in the distant part of a vast farming 'property'. Reporters from around the

---

[31] 4,041 kilometres

world had gathered there, but the farmer who owned the property said, "I only go to that part of the property once a year, and I'm far too busy to go there now!" To Adelaide across the Nullarbor desert were stretches of straight road that went on for a hundred and fifty kilometres. They visited the old gold-mining town of Ballarat, and at their camp in Healesville, outside Melbourne, they enjoyed seeing a platypus in an aquarium. On the road to Sydney they passed the statue (made famous by an Australian song) of the 'Dog on the tucker-box; nine miles from Gundagai'. They visited the scenic Blue Mountains and climbed Mount Kosciusko, the highest peak in Australia, walking through snow near the top!

Later in that year I wrote:

> *We thank God their trip was trouble-free. Bruce has finished his first year at university studying Psychology, Anthropology, Philosophy and English. Far from the subjects putting him on the Christian defensive, he has found many opportunities for thrilling Christian witness. Tim has been chosen to be one of the two Australian delegates at an international Christian students' conference to be held in England in July 1983, with travel paid.*

At that time, in his hospital work, Stewart was told of spiral bacteria that had been seen microscopically for many years on the surface of the stomach but had never been grown in a microbiology laboratory. Stewart was asked to allocate extra staff time and materials to try to grow these bacteria, but there was no research money for this project. As Stewart was always keen to help other researchers, he did ask his staff to try to grow these bacteria, using a much wider range of culture methods. In the first thirty-four specimens, spiral bacteria were not found; but finally, in April 1982, Stewart's staff grew the 'bug' (probably for the first time in the world), and from many patients after that. It was initially called *Campylobacter pyloridis*.

A clinical colleague studied the hospital notes of the patients in whom the bug was found and noted it occurred most commonly in patients with duodenal ulcer. But Stewart was never told about this, and then for the last six months of 1983 we were on sabbatical leave in Canada. While we were away, a paper appeared in the Lancet medical journal about the discovery! In due course, Stewart helped his colleagues to discover that antibiotic treatment for only two or three weeks would cure duodenal ulcer. Up till then, patients had to take anti-acid drugs for all their lives, to relieve the pain and avoid life-threatening bleeding from the ulcer.

Stewart had recently done research on the unique chemical pattern of the cell-walls of bacteria that distinguishes each genus or family of bacteria. In January 1984, he tested this new bug and was thrilled to find that its chemical pattern showed it was in a different genus from every other known bug in the world. He obtained research grants, and from 1984 he and his microbiology team studied the bug and published thirty scientific papers on it. He slowly obtained the many other proofs that are required to justify naming a new genus, which is much more significant than naming a new species. Finally, in 1989 he startled the medical and microbiological world when he announced this new genus and the name he gave it – *Helicobacter;* he named the bug *Helicobacter pylori.*

From 1985, after his first research papers, requests for lectures by him came flooding in, and I travelled with him to many countries. During our travels around the USA and Canada, we took the opportunity to stay in Vancouver, where I have many nieces and nephews and their families. My two elder sisters had emigrated to Canada soon after the Second World War, and they both had had several children. I loved renewing family ties, and we enjoyed happy times with them. We also visited friends who had been in Chefoo School with us and in camp under the Japanese, with many memories to share. As a child I had seen postcards of the Grand Canyon which my father had visited, and I always longed to go there. Fortunately, on one lecture tour we had the opportunity to visit it, staying first in Las Vegas for a night. Standing on the edge of the huge Canyon, we watched rain sweep in, followed by a wonderful rainbow. We enjoyed a 3-D film of the earliest white people who had travelled by raft down the Colorado River, a mile down at the base of the Canyon.

In early 1984, Ruth started work in Canberra in the Overseas Aid Department of the Australian Government, and in due course was sent to Ethiopia to oversee and distribute Australian aid in the terrible famine there. Caroline had gone to live permanently in England in 1983 and was doing private-practice and hospital nursing. She visited Stewart's parents frequently. Meanwhile, Tim joined 'Youth With A

Mission' (YWAM) in England and then went on Christian 'missions' to Europe and Israel. Bruce had become Vice President of the University Christian Union, leading a Bible study group in the Arts Faculty.

We made a point of travelling to England every year, for a medical conference or during one of Stewart's lecture tours, and always spent several days with Stewart's parents in Sussex. They remained living happily in their own bungalow, and Stewart's father loved his gardening. Then in November 1984, we received a phone call from Stewart's father that his mother had suddenly died. Stewart immediately flew to England for the funeral, and the burial was in the beautiful churchyard of Bodiam where Stewart's grandfather had been Rector and where Stewart had lived for two years from the age of six while his parents were in China.

Stewart's father remained very well in his own home; but in April 1985, after going out to lunch, he died suddenly of a heart attack. Very sadly, Stewart was forbidden by his surgeon to travel back to England, as in February he had undergone a major operation on his lower back.[32] Fortunately, Timothy and Caroline were in Europe and were able to go to the funeral, and Timothy read Stewart's tribute to his father. By July, Stewart was able to go to England after a conference in Ottawa and helped clear up his parents' home. He retrieved all the letters that he had written to his parents since the age of thirteen, which his mother had kept.

In September 1985, we celebrated Bruce's twenty-first birthday, and it was lovely that Ruth, Tim and Caroline were all able to return to Perth for the occasion.

Our memorable visit to China

In 1986, Stewart was invited to lecture for six weeks on *Helicobacter pylori* and its treatment, in various Chinese cities, starting in September. It would be a marvellous opportunity to see so much of this great country, which had been our 'home' as children for thirteen years. First, we flew to Hong Kong for one night to contact Christian friends, who provided us with a Chinese Bible to

---

[32] As a result of the years of malnutrition as a prisoner of the Japanese, Stewart's back had given him severe pain in his left leg since 1962.

take to a doctor in Shanghai. It would be a risk to us if a Bible was found in our luggage, but God protected us. We then flew on to Beijing to start our tour, and a 'minder' accompanied us in each city. The doctors welcomed the up-to-date information that Stewart brought about *H. pylori* and its role in duodenal ulcer and stomach cancer.

In Beijing, between Stewart's lectures, we enjoyed visiting the main sights, including the Great Wall. In the next stop, Jinan, we visited a traditional medicine Chinese hospital and saw acupuncture, 'cupping', and a doctor massaging a baby boy's thumb to  cure his diarrhoea. From there, we took the overnight train to where I was born, Chefoo – now called Yantai. So much was recognisable even after forty-five years away – the beach, and rocks and sea wall, and the school compound which was now a Naval Academy, where we were not allowed. I remembered the mimosa trees and pink tamarisk, and bitter-sweet memories came flooding back. We visited the three small houses on Temple Hill where a hundred and fifty of us had been imprisoned during the Second World War for a year.

Then on to Shanghai, where again the memories came flooding back – familiar road names and the sea front with the famous huge Bund buildings, built before the Second World War. But now the pavements were absolutely packed with people, and the roads with bicycles. September in China is called 'the Golden Autumn' and we had good weather throughout our stay, except for one day in Shanghai when there was the most enormous thunderstorm. This was the day that we intended to give the Bible to the Shanghai doctor. The lobby of the hotel was packed full of people escaping the rain, and our efficient minder was waiting there. To our surprise, when somebody knocked at the door of our room, it was the Chinese Christian doctor on his own. We welcomed him in, gave him the Bible and prayed together, just before another knock and our minder appeared. It must have been a miracle that our minder had failed to observe the doctor in the hall.

The next day we went to a shop where I saw curiously-shaped porcelain pieces, in delicate colours characteristic of old Chinese culture, made into brooches, pendants and rings.

I asked the old Chinese man behind the counter, "Why are these items such unusual shapes?" During a long pause he looked at me, so I said, "I was born and brought up in China."

He said, "During the terrible days of the Cultural Revolution, Red Guards smashed the wonderful Ming vases. I and others collected up what could be salvaged and made them into these curiously-shaped pieces."

I nearly wept with him; it was such a moving account. I came away with a now much-treasured pendant.

Hangzhou was our next city, where Stewart had been brought up. A senior Chinese doctor met us who had played with Stewart when they were small boys together. We visited the beautiful West Lake, with its stone-arch bridges, moon-shaped gates, and floating lotus flowers. Next was the inland city of Guilin, with its small conical mountains and the meandering Li River. In the early morning mist, we went on a boat down the river, and saw water buffaloes in the river meadows and unique cormorants on small rafts, trained for catching fish for their owners; then on to Chongqing, in the far-west Sichuan province, where we enjoyed seeing giant pandas and the much smaller red pandas.

From Chongqing we took the river journey down towards the coast through the Yangtze Gorges, a journey my grandfather had done many times during his forty years in China from 1885. We had a fabulous view of the dramatic, steep-sided Gorges, and could still see tow-paths carved into the rocky sides that had been used by humans and horses to pull boats up and down the river for thousands of years before boats were motorised.

After three days the boat reached Wuhan, where we attended a banquet, and a senior heart surgeon sat next to us, who was a Christian and had suffered much during the ten years of the Cultural Revolution. It was a pleasant surprise when he was asked to offer a prayer before our meal. Before we left Wuhan, our guide, who spoke Mandarin, telephoned the person due to meet us in Canton, who spoke Cantonese; but our guide got more and more infuriated. Finally, he slammed down the phone and said, "Stupid man, he can't speak Chinese!" Consequently, when we arrived at Canton airport the next day there was no one to meet us. Also, the Queen of Great Britain was visiting Canton that very day, so every hotel room was full. We could speak enough Cantonese to take a taxi and, very fortunately, found a free bedroom in the Public Health building.

Finally, back to Hong Kong and a decent cup of coffee, which was very welcome after only green tea in China. I was sitting in a coffee-shop, looking out onto the pavement, and saw a pregnant Chinese woman walking along the street holding her small son by the hand. Without thinking, I said to Stewart, "She already has one child. She is not supposed to be pregnant again!" I suddenly realised what I'd said and was horrified to realise how, after our many weeks in China, I had absorbed their 'one child policy'. We enjoyed two days in Hong Kong, finding the old shops in the backstreets on the Island selling real old Chinese ware, before finally returning home to WA.

In June 1987, Stewart lectured in Berlin, before the Berlin Wall had been removed. It was exciting to fly up the Berlin 'air-corridor' to the old German capital, divided in half between the West and the East but surrounded by communist East Germany. In one city square the stark ruins of a bombed-out church was a reminder of the Second World War, but the Linden trees were all blossoming.

When Ruth returned from Ethiopia to Canberra, I travelled from Perth by train to spend time with her. During the three days and three nights across the Nullarbor Desert, the landscape was empty and desolate, but I enjoyed the beautiful scenery in the Blue Mountains in New South Wales. From England, Caroline wrote to us:

> I have stopped nursing to join a Christian Theatre company (Stripes Theatre). Our material is original with plays about homelessness, leprosy, AIDS, a satirical revue, and Christian sketches. We launched an appeal for a new van, and amazingly our prayers were answered as we were given £5,000 in two months.

In June 1988, Stewart lectured in the USA, and we stopped in Hawaii, where Bruce was training with YWAM, and we were glad to spend time with him there. After training, he was sent to the Cook Islands in the South Pacific, where it was wonderful to be involved in a Christian revival. He then led a small team of ten people to the

Philippines. In 1989, he worked for a year with YWAM in Calcutta and spent a short time at Mother Teresa's orphanage.

My biggest challenge was when Stewart was invited to lecture again in Japan, in March 1989. On his previous visit to Japan, I had refused to go, as I still felt very bitter about the war. This time, our four children decided I really *needed* to go. Eventually, after much thought and prayer, I decided to go with him. I found the Japanese medical people to be quite different from the Japanese military, who had invaded my youth and filled my memories; but arriving at Tokyo Airport was a nightmare for me, with everyone talking Japanese. However, our hosts were kind and polite, and I had to overcome my fears.

Our chief host was a Professor in Tokyo, and one evening he invited Stewart and me out to a meal at a Geisha Club! We were collected from our hotel by limousine, but during the drive I hastily looked at my invitation to make sure that I also had been invited, and I found I was the only woman guest there. We sat down at a low table, which fortunately had a lowered floor below it so that our legs could sit normally. Each of us had a charming and beautiful Geisha girl at our side – Stewart had the most beautiful one! Each dish came on a different style of plate, such as a little house on the corner, and the plate matched the food that was being served. The entertainment at the end was in the traditional Noh style, performed by an older, single Japanese woman in a white mask. It certainly was a fascinating experience, and I wonder how many other non-Japanese women have been invited to such a club.

On a lecture trip later in 1989 to Sydney, Melbourne and Adelaide, we diverted to Alice Springs and then to Ayer's Rock, now known as Uluru. At that time, it was still permitted for people to climb to the top of the Rock, which we found to be a surprisingly large plateau with an undulating surface. Around the bottom of the Rock are many intriguing caves, some of which we investigated. In the past they were used for ancient Aboriginal celebrations. We watched the colours of Ayers Rock change as the sun set – from its unique red colour to purple, to very dark. Visiting the Rock felt like a finale to our Australian sojourn, as another major development in our lives was about to occur.

By 1989, our four children had left Perth for various reasons, and it did not seem likely that they would return to settle down in Perth. Then our beloved retriever, Casper, died. I was devastated, as he had been my constant companion and confidant. The University Microbiology Department started demanding more from Stewart in the way of teaching, but this would mean less time for his research, although he had obtained several large grants to do research on *H. pylori*. It was not a happy situation.

At the end of 1988, a visiting professor friend from England had told Stewart about a new Medical School in the United Arab Emirates (UAE), in the city of Al Ain, inland from Abu Dhabi; the School was looking for talented staff. We hardly knew where the UAE was, and we were not sure we wanted to live in the Middle East. However, in April 1989, Stewart was telephoned from the UAE: "Dr Goodwin, we would like to offer you the post of Head of Bacteriology in the Medical School, and with your wife to pay a visit to Al Ain, with all expenses paid." We prayed a lot and decided, "Why not?"

With Bruce working in India, we arranged to stop in Delhi, to spend a little time with him. He would fly to Delhi from Calcutta. To my shame, while we were sitting at Delhi airport waiting for him, I did not recognise my son until he was close to me. He had been ill, lost a lot of weight and was wearing Indian clothes. The next day, all three of us went on the train to see the Taj Mahal, which we found absolutely beautiful.

Stewart and I flew on to the UAE, and next to me on the plane was an American lady who had been in India buying textiles. As we passed over mile after mile of empty desert, she said to me, "Are you sure you want to live here?" It certainly looked very barren. We landed in Abu Dhabi Airport and took a taxi the hundred miles inland into the desert, to the little town of Al Ain. Stewart found the new Medical School to be well-run, and the professors were mainly from the UK. I met some of the university staff wives and asked about the intricacies of living as a Westerner in a small but westernised city in a relatively relaxed Muslim country. I was glad to learn that expatriate women were allowed to drive in the UAE.

Our visit included a Friday. This is the Muslim holy day and the weekly holiday, so the Christian Community had their Christian Service on Friday, not Sunday. We attended the church which was run by an American pastor – in the grounds of a small Christian Mission hospital in Al Ain. We were welcomed at the service, and thus we were reassured that it was possible to enjoy Christian worship there every week. The whole prospect of the job and life in the UAE seemed worthwhile.

Back in Perth, it was decision time. I had not been really happy in Australia and had very few close friends. The thought of a new country, with new opportunities for both of us, was exciting. We had coffee with David, the minister of our church. While sitting on the lawn in his garden, we asked his opinion. He listened with interest to our description of Al Ain, and his reaction was, "Go for it!" So we did – after much thought and prayer. Particularly as all our family had left Perth, we decided that this was the right move. With two members of our family in England at the time, living in the Middle East would bring us much closer to them. We would buy a flat in London, in which our son and daughter could live, and we would go there for the summer holidays, as the temperature in the UAE could reach 50°C – too hot to live comfortably.

Prior to our eventual move in January 1990, it was fortunate that in September 1989 Stewart had two lecture engagements in England with three weeks in between, and we could look for a flat to purchase. Our daughter was at the time living in Wimbledon, and we went to have a look at the area. We liked the wonderful Common and found that Wimbledon had excellent train links to London. After looking at several properties we found a suitable flat – three bedrooms, two bathrooms, bath and shower, and on the first floor – all we had prayed for. Caroline and Timothy moved in, and Bruce joined them when he returned from India. In December we sold our house in Perth, packed everything up, shipped our heavy luggage back to England, and left Australia. For our last two nights we stayed with a couple from church, and one evening had a wonderful farewell gathering with many church friends.

CHAPTER NINE

1990-96, on the edge of the desert in the United Arab Emirates; travels in the Middle East – in Yemen my driver needed a Kalashnikov!

*a*fter our years in Australia, we now looked forward to a new phase in our life in a different country and culture, but with the bonus of a base in England, where we could see more of our family. This was the sixth country we had lived in! Living in a country is quite different from paying a brief visit. We left Australia in mid-December 1989 and could not resist stopping for two days in Hong Kong on our way to London. In the middle of January, Stewart flew out to the UAE to take up his position in the new Medical School in Al Ain. I had to remain in London to oversee the arrival of our household luggage from Australia. Bruce, after a year in India, arranged to stop in Al Ain for a few months before returning to England. Stewart was glad of his companionship.

The UAE is composed of seven Emirates – each ruled by its own Emir – that combined to form the country in 1972. As Abu Dhabi is the largest Emirate and has vast reserves of oil, the President of the UAE is always the Emir of Abu Dhabi Emirate. In our day this was Sheikh Zayed, a wise ruler with unlimited power. The city of Al Ain lies in the Abu Dhabi Emirate, 160 km inland of Abu Dhabi, where Sheikh Zayed founded the UAE University. Al Ain has been in existence for thousands of years, because of a large natural oasis. When we were there, there was a limited variety of shops, and for anything sophisticated, or a wider range of foods, we had to go to Dubai (120 km) or Abu Dhabi. We were glad to live in Al Ain because it had a low humidity, in contrast to the coastal cities that are humid. Thus, in the very hot summers, we found the heat in Al Ain was bearable but did not go out for our daily walk until the sun had set.

Before I arrived, Stewart met an Arab man who told him, "There is as much immorality in this country as in a Western country," and we heard stories about UAE men and women to confirm this. Also, their Philippino maids were frequently abused. A man could divorce one of his four wives by saying three times, "I divorce you." All children belonged to their father, unless he allowed the divorced wife to take them.

I arrived in Al Ain in February. We were able to choose a quiet university flat and felt fortunate to have large spacious rooms, good air conditioning and underground parking. This latter was much appreciated during the hot, hot (45°C) days, as it prevented the car being too hot when I got in to it. Very few of the university blocks of flats had such underground parking. When we moved into our flat, it was situated right on the edge of the Arabian Desert, and all we saw were undulating dunes stretching uninterrupted away for miles. The size and height of some of these dunes were incredible. The changing colours of the sand at dawn and sunset were beautiful – an unending source of delight. We watched camels wandering past in the desert, often with a small boy looking after them.

Camels in the desert

The Arab women were all clothed in black and most were veiled. However, 85% of the population in the UAE were immigrant workers from many countries in the Far East and the Middle East. As we were now living in a Muslim country and needed to respect their customs and dress codes, I was careful to dress in the proper way – a loose, long top with sleeves and baggy trousers. But I found it quite an ordeal visiting the various officials in their offices. The Muslim men had a habit of not acknowledging women at all, which I found very disconcerting. There were so many new things to get accustomed to – the heat, the call of the muezzins five times a day starting at dawn, and the men who could not get to a mosque stopping in the street on their prayer mats to pray at the time the muezzins called. During the month of Ramadan between dawn and dusk, eating and drinking in a public place is forbidden; night is when people eat and socialise. In the hot weather, after drivers had not eaten or drunk all day, we found that the driving was very erratic, and we were especially careful – one car appeared to have tried to go up a palm tree! This fasting month occurs on a different date each year as it depends on the lunar calendar.

Life for us settled down. The Medical School was just starting, and so there were not too many 'university wives', and we could get to know each other. There were coffee mornings, a craft group and an exercise group. The Medical School was run on strict Islamic lines. The girl students were taught in different classes from the male students. They lived in segregated hostels and were taken in darkened buses to the lecture halls. Stewart had to give every lecture twice. However, in classes they were not veiled, as Stewart and other lecturers were not UAE citizens. Interestingly, four years later Stewart noticed that as soon as the students finished their medical course and started working in a hospital, men and women worked alongside each other. Most UAE marriages occurred between first cousins, but this could lead to one or more of their children having mental deficiencies. When Stewart asked the girls why this custom persisted, they answered, "When my husband beats me, my father can appeal to his brother to stop it."

When Stewart gave the lecture on the 'tail' possessed by some bacteria, he took the opportunity to say that the Latin name for this – 'flagellum' – is the same word used for the whip used to whip Jesus before he was crucified. This led on to some conversations after the lecture. Two or three students asked to be given a New Testament, but this had to be done very secretly.

On one occasion, the wife of the Dean of the Medical School asked me to "look after the wife" of a visiting American professor. I agreed and dutifully drove her around Al Ain and up Jebel Hafeet, which was our local mountain. The new road up it was good, but steep and winding, and from the top the views were amazing in all directions: sand dunes stretching for miles. From the top, we could also see at the foot of our mountain the original, age-old oasis of Al Ain with its water and lush greenery. Our visitor was interested and quite impressed. However, to my surprise, I was told later, "That lady is certainly married but not to the visiting professor that she came with!" The professor did not accept a post in Al Ain.

During our years in the UAE, we usually arrived back on a flight from Heathrow to Dubai late at night. The taxi ride out to Al Ain was a real pleasure – a warm, starry night – and the lights on the road up to Jebel Hafeet seemed to hang in the air, resembling 'Jacob's Ladder', as described in the Bible book of Genesis. We could see these lights from quite a distance away and then knew we were nearly 'home'.

At the time, the two big hotels in Al Ain were the Hilton and Intercontinental. Both had large swimming pools, with excellent attendants and changing rooms. I love swimming and was able enjoy a swim before breakfast almost every day, as we lived only a few minutes' drive from the Hilton Hotel.

There was a small Christian hospital in Al Ain, called the Oasis Hospital, which had been founded thirty years earlier when there was no hospital in Al Ain, and the current ruler of Abu Dhabi had invited American doctors to come. Inside the hospital grounds was a small Christian church hall, where we had our weekly Friday evening service. Some of UAE women had as many as fifteen pregnancies and consequently needed the care of the hospital. As I am a nurse, I was glad to help voluntarily in the Ante-natal Department of the hospital, monitoring the pre-natal women, which I much enjoyed. The women were friendly and appreciative. Some of us nurses working in the department would be invited to visit them back in their villages. We all sat on cushions and drank coffee with them out of tiny cups without handles – a real ritual. All their children were running around.

The neighbouring country of Oman has a fascinating culture with a long history. It had been a kingdom for many hundreds of years with established cities and used to rule the island of Zanzibar. However, from about 1850 the country had bad rulers and became very poor. When the current ruler, Sultan Qaboos, took power from his father in 1972, there was only five kilometres of paved road in the country and no schools except for those attached to mosques. He did a marvellous job using the moderate amount of oil revenues to modernise the country, bringing education to boys and girls and creating a fine university, a modern infrastructure and excellent roads.

The border between the UAE and Oman opened for the first time to tourists only in 1990, and so we went for a weekend. On the way to the capital Muscat, we turned off to a fishing village and saw their simple boats drawn up on the sand, and the fishermen pulling in their nets by hand, full of large, wet fish. We felt we had gone back in time. In Oman, the women seemed to have more freedom than in other Gulf countries; their full-length dresses and head-coverings were of colourful material, and they were natural and friendly. On beautiful Muttrah bay near Muscat we visited the traditional market or 'souk', with a large range of local products for sale: wood carvings, a kaleidoscope of colourful cloth garments and scarves, traditional silver jewellery, and horn-handled daggers known as 'khunjars'. These are still worn by Omani men, tucked into their belt in the centre of their stomach, as the Sultan encourages people to wear traditional clothes.

Hauling fishing nets on the Oman coast

Stewart and I went to Oman again that year – in June – when he was invited to be an examiner in the University Medical School. We drove a different way into the country, through the inland city of Nizwa where we visited the old souk, which was mainly inside a cave. There were no other tourists there, and as we came out, an obviously deranged man was waving a huge sword around. Fortunately, he did not see our white faces!

On one of the Omani beaches, turtles return every year at exactly the same time to bury their eggs in deep holes, cover them up and lumber back to the sea. We were fortunate to go to that beach a few years later, when our son Bruce was working in Oman, and we watched the turtles lay their eggs; and from some of the older nests we saw baby turtles trying to find their way down to the edge of the water. Another year, Bruce drove us to the Oman-owned Musandam

Peninsula at the mouth of the Arabian Gulf, through the Musandam mountains to the coast, finally reaching the deeply indented coastline known as the Fjords of Oman. We stayed in the chief town, Khorsab, and early one morning we booked a local dhow to take us out on the fjords and up the inlets. With the sun low on the water, we were accompanied by dolphins that played around the boat. It was absolutely beautiful.

Every summer, we went back to our flat in England for the university holidays during July and August. In 1990, we were delighted to be in England when Caroline was married to Nick McIvor – a memorable and very happy day. Nick's Scottish family flew down from Glasgow and impressed us with their kilts and sporrans. It was the first time all six of us in our family had been together for five years. Ruth came from Boston, USA, where she had just finished her first year at Harvard Business School.

In July, Stewart received a telephone call from our inter-denominational church in the UAE, telling him that a new pastor who was due to come in September could not come. Stewart was asked to be the acting pastor in the church for the next nine months. We had been going to that church only since January, but Stewart said that if they felt he could do the job, he would be happy to do it. Of course, Stewart had been very active in churches ever since his Cambridge University days from 1951, so he was used to being 'up front' and leading congregations.

Then in August 1990, the Iraqi ruler Saddam Hussein invaded Kuwait. As it did not seem likely that the Iraqi Army would travel down the coast to the UAE, we duly returned there in September, but Stewart's excellent secretary took fright and refused to come back from her leave in Europe. I took a bracelet to be mended in a shop, which was full of gold jewellery. But on returning to the shop a few days later, I found it was empty of all its gold! The Arab women regard their jewellery as their investment, and they had bought up all the gold they could find. This was a strange and unusual time, but life went on at the university. Students had their lectures, and the hospitals continued treating local patients, even though there was a great feeling of unease. Many rumours circulated of illicit weapons being smuggled into Al Ain; and in case the Iraqi Army came south from Kuwait, there was an evacuation plan for us to go into Oman. However, fortunately this did not become necessary.

Ruth, after her first year at Harvard, felt she needed time off from her studies and started her vacation by coming just before Christmas 1990 to stay with us in the UAE. She was there when the United Nations forces started the Gulf War against Iraq, and wrote in her diary:

January 15, 1991 is imprinted in my mind, as the deadline to Saddam Hussein passed. We know there are eight hundred kilometres and the most powerful army in the world between us and the Iraqi army in Kuwait. Despite knowing this, the fear is tangible. Every dinner party and casual conversation turns to war. Prayer becomes an acceptable conversation topic.

January 17th: War in the Gulf started today at 2:30 a.m. when I was sound asleep. I woke to discover that the Australian and British wardens appointed in Al Ain had called to tell us to stay inside. I ignored such ridiculous advice! As I went around town today, I discovered that the authorities had closed public facilities such as the zoo and museums.

January 19: Life is now almost back to normal in Al Ain. The fear has gone. We are officially allowed to go out but have been warned of possible terrorist attacks. When I watch CNN TV, I note that all references to Israel and possible Israeli responses to Iraqi Scud missile attacks are censored. So we get a three-minute silent view of Abu Dhabi instead. The UAE government does not recognise the state of Israel. On the other hand, the Palestinians and Jordanians who are working here want to see the results of Saddam's missiles hitting Israel, because they are gleeful when it occurs.

When Saddam Hussein set fire to the oil wells in Kuwait, we could see the black smoke even from the UAE.

The USA Army erected a big base just outside Al Ain, beside the huge Al Ain airfield; it was one of the biggest in the Middle East – built by Sheikh Zayed. Some of the US soldiers came to our services, and we warmly welcomed them. Many of them felt lonely, having left their families behind in the USA. At Christmas time, we were invited to a special concert the soldiers gave at their camp. Every car was carefully checked that it was not carrying any guns or bombs into the camp. When the soldiers had to leave at the end of the Gulf War, it was sad to say farewell to those who had come to our services.

My brother Jim also came to visit us at Christmas 1990 and stayed with us for a month. In early January, before the Gulf War started, we drove with him and Ruth into Oman, and he really loved our tour. We stopped in an inland village to look at the underground and overground water channels (the ancient 'falaj' system) and arrived in the middle of a colourful wedding procession; we were warmly welcomed. We visited the ancient city of Sur, where the traditional boats – 'dhows' – have been made by hand on the beaches probably for thousands of years; the trade-winds can take such boats to India and back. A very marked feature of inland Oman, and especially the desert Bedouin, was that the women wore heavy face-masks, different to what we had seen in the UAE.

Ruth with an Omani Bedouin woman

Jim was due to return to England just after the start of the first Gulf War, flying from Dubai airport. We lived a hundred miles inland from Dubai, and no cars were supposed to travel at that time. However, he had to reach the airport – so we drove anyway! It was a deserted road and a deserted airport. Fortunately there was still one flight out, which was routed south away from the Gulf War, and then to Athens and on to London.

Ruth stayed with us for four months and enjoyed the Natural History Group energetic walks in the neighbouring mountains between the UAE and Oman, seeing the rare mountain gazelle and ancient, isolated villages. She graduated with a Distinction from Harvard in June 1992, and Stewart took up an invitation he had had to lecture in Boston. We were delighted to attend her graduation ceremony – twenty-five thousand people under the trees in a four hour ceremony, and Stewart in his scarlet Cambridge MD robes.

Near our flat lived an interesting woman from Somalia. She had won a beauty contest in her home country, at a time when extreme Muslim views did not dominate society there. Not only was she beautiful but she had a nice character. However, she found life in Al Ain was restrictive compared to Somalia, where she had freedom to dress in a short skirt and did not need to cover her head with a scarf. She avoided the enveloping black robe worn by all Arab women in the UAE. I went to tea in their home, and she also visited me for coffee with her youngest child – a very engaging and mischievous young fellow, with curly hair and big brown eyes. She was happy to come to a small weekly Bible study that I had with some of our friends, but sadly, one day she just took her children and left Al Ain without telling her husband. She flew off to Canada for a new life.

During our early years in Al Ain, two Iranian young men turned up in our church one Friday. One had been training to become a mullah[33] in the north of Iran; the other was from the south of their country. They both had become disillusioned with Islam and, amazingly, had each been given a copy of the New Testament and determined that they would become Christians. This meant that in Iran their lives were in danger. They had each escaped to the UAE, where they had met and come to the inland city of Al Ain – as they felt it was safer there for them as Christians who had been Muslims. We had many fascinating conversations with them, and their experience of Jesus as their Saviour and friend contrasted with their experience of Islam. They explained to us that the Koranic teachings about Allah are totally different from those describing our God (Father, Son and Holy Spirit) in the Bible, and in their experience.

---

[33] Muslim 'priest'

172

They were adamant that the names 'Allah' and 'God' are not interchangeable.

As they only had UN refugee visas they desperately needed to get to a country that would not deport them back to Iran. We suggested that they use our home fax machine to make contact with the US embassy in Istanbul to obtain visas to go to the USA, although this was somewhat risky for us. With their temporary visas, the only airline that would take them was Yugoslav Airlines. On the plane to Belgrade, they were horrified to hear the pilot announcing that, due to fighting in Belgrade, he would have to return to the UAE. Fortunately, they were allowed to speak to the pilot and explained to him that, if they returned, they would be sent on to Iran and might lose their lives. Miraculously, the pilot decided he could divert to Istanbul and was given clearance to land there. One can imagine what a relief this was for them. In Istanbul, one met and married a Swedish girl, and they now live in Sweden. The other duly went to the USA and became a Christian pastor.

Into our church one day came a man from Oman. Stewart told him about the Holy Spirit, who is unknown among Muslims, and soon he became a Christian. He was not shy about his faith, and very sadly, a few years later he was run over and died.

After the Muslim holy month of Ramadan, there was the three-day Eid holiday, when it was a tradition to visit those in authority. Once, with other ladies from the Oasis Hospital, I was invited to visit the mother of the Crown Prince of Abu Dhabi, in his palace in the centre of Al Ain. I was lent a long Arab dress, with ornate embroidery round the neck and cuffs of the sleeves. We went in a convoy of six cars and swept into the main gates of the palace. There were beautiful lawns and gardens and, inside, a predominance of enormous gold chandeliers. In the meeting room (the 'majlis') we met the old lady – the first wife of Sheikh Zayed, now divorced – and then were ushered into another large room and sat on the floor. We were faced with dishes piled high with rice and lamb, and oatmeal and minced meat mixed together. It was all rather difficult to eat with our fingers but was tasty and followed by fruit and exotic sweetmeats. In the corridors, we passed men dressed in new, white, long robes and headdresses, wearing daggers tucked into their belts, no doubt guarding the palace and everyone in it. I would not have missed this opportunity, even to drinking numerous cups of Arabic coffee and knowing to 'waggle' my cup (which means, "No more, thank you!")

Soon after that we joined a group of friends on a day's trip on a dhow boat off the coast that faced the Indian Ocean, in an area where the coast is very dramatic, with steep, bare mountains plunging down into the clear blue sea. The dhow stopped several times so we could jump off the boat and go swimming in the warm sea. It was a wonderful day.

While Stewart was in charge of the Al Ain church he started two traditions which everyone said made the services more interesting. Each week, he spoke for five minutes about an important Christian person who had lived in the last two thousand years, including people we knew who were currently working in interesting and dangerous places, bringing the Gospel of Jesus to the local people. One American lady said, "You must write a book with these stories in it!" Each month, Stewart asked someone who attended the church to tell us "what Jesus means to me". One was a Muslim man from Bangladesh who had come to Al Ain to start a small business. He found the local UAE people were reluctant or late to pay their bills, while Christians were always prompt in paying. He decided to find out more about Christianity and came to our church, where he heard about Jesus and believed in Him. Stewart also started a morning service on Fridays, which was more convenient for families with young children. A new pastor arrived in mid-1991.

We got to know a wonderful young Pakistani man called Richard, who had become a very ardent Christian. Having been illiterate, when Jesus became his Saviour, he opened the Bible and found he could read simple words! God worked in miraculous ways for Richard, which he told us about when he came to pray with us every month. Stewart had given him a telephone card to be able to phone his family in Pakistan – to speak for twenty minutes – but he found he could speak for much longer than that, for many months, before the card eventually ran out. On another occasion, he was returning to Pakistan to get married and he would be expected to bring many presents for all his relatives in his and his bride's families. Stewart gave him a certain amount of money in an envelope, which he carried to numerous shops in the town. He kept on taking money out of the envelope, and when he told us what he had bought, it was quite obvious it was many times what Stewart had put in the envelope!

In 1992, a famous Muslim mosque in Ayodhya, India – constructed in 1527 by the first Mughal Emperor – was demolished by Hindu crowds. This led to great unrest in India but also anger among the many Muslim workmen in the UAE from Pakistan. In Al Ain, a large mob marched through the streets with sticks, shouting their defiance, and trashed a small Roman Catholic church. Richard belonged to a small Pentecostal church situated in the area where the Pakistani workmen lived, and the mob decided they would destroy his church, as representing a foreign religion. Richard was equally determined to save it! While a friend stayed outside, he shut himself into the small building and started praying very earnestly. He heard fierce shouting outside, but he felt the Holy Spirit pushing him down onto his knees.

Suddenly, there was a deadly hush. Richard got up, went to see his friend and asked, "What has happened?"

His friend replied, "You won't believe this, but 'bullets of fire' came out from the church, which made the crowd very frightened, and they all ran away!"

One man's prayers and God's power saved that little church.

All of our children came to visit us in the UAE at one time or another. It was lovely to take them to areas where all they saw was sand in every direction, and then we would come upon a small household where an old man was looking after his camels. One student of Stewart's said that his elderly father refused to leave his desert home, because he said it was far healthier than in a city. In the centre of Al Ain there was a camel market that had probably been in existence for four thousand years. Camels were brought in by Bedouin from the surrounding desert and sold in the middle of the town. It was a remarkable sight to see camels of all ages, sizes and colours. When two friends from Australia visited us, we all went riding on camels in the desert, as this was possible from Al Ain. We mounted when the camel was sitting on the sand, but we had to hang on tightly when the camel got up. When riding, it was a very 'swaying' motion!

After living for some time in Al Ain, we heard that camel races were held on the outskirts of the town. Each time we went, we were the only Westerners at the track. So whenever we had visiting friends, we would take them to the races, which were a wonderful insight into Bedouin life – "Arabs at play". They arrived in four-wheel drives wearing their white 'dish-dashas', and many with a falcon perched on their forearm. We also watched the camel 'trains' (lines of camels) appearing over the sand dunes and then had the excitement of the race on a well-kept racecourse. The track was about two miles long, and the centre was completely grassed, which had to be kept watered in the terrific heat. It was always an amazing experience, well worth seeing.

One of the delights of living in the UAE was exploring the souks in each city. The Sharjah souk had a particularly fine range of carpets, many from Iran. Needless to say, my good friend Dorothy and I each bought one or two carpets, which have adorned our homes ever since. For the first few years we were in the UAE, prices of Iranians carpets were relatively cheap, as Americans were forbidden to purchase items from Iran, after their embassy staff had been taken hostage in the country. For the most part, we found the Emirates an easy place in which to live. In Dubai, we explored the old parts of the city where they had preserved ancient 'wind towers' that had been built to provide cool air before air conditioning was available. In that area were narrow alleyways, from where small boats[34] would ferry people across the estuary to the souks on the other side. The gold souk and the spice market, with colourful sacks of peppers, were still housed in old buildings.

In August 1993, Bruce married Jo in the beautiful West Country town of Broadway, on a lovely sunny day. Everything had been planned meticulously by Jo and her parents; she looked marvellous. My brother Jim, who lived not far away, made a supreme effort to come, and loved the service. He had been very sick since March. Two days after the wedding he died peacefully. Jim had been teaching for a year in Shanghai, up to mid-1992, where he climbed mountains faster than people half his age. Very sadly, my only other brother, Lionel, suddenly became very ill at the end of September, and he died in October. He had a great concern for the underprivileged including

---

[34] 'abras'

those in developing countries and had been a much respected senior master at Sherborne School for many years.

Earlier in August, Ruth had got engaged to Paul, a tall American. They flew over from New York for Bruce and Jo's wedding and were in Wimbledon for a week. We much enjoyed meeting and getting to know Paul. His parents had been Christian workers in Nigeria, and Paul hoped to make a career of opera singing. Ruth was working for Women's World Banking in New York and had to travel worldwide frequently. In January 1994, Ruth married Paul in York. All our family arrived from London during the preceding week. We found New York exceptionally cold but glistening, with snow on the ground. It was nice to meet Paul's parents and some of his relations.

Later that year, Stewart did his first lecture tour in the Middle East. He was in demand to teach doctors how to use antibiotics in the best way, as some bacteria have hidden resistance to commonly-used antibiotics, which can be detected by a laboratory technique he used.

My friend Dorothy was able to come with us, so I had company while Stewart was lecturing. During our first stop in Cyprus, we visited a Crusader Castle in a magnificent position on a headland. The next stop was Amman, capital of Jordan. Stewart lectured in two hospitals; and then we were taken to the wonderful city of Petra, a four-hour car journey from Amman. Having read so much about the 'Rose-Red city', it was amazing to go there. In Petra, a horse-drawn carriage took us through the narrow 'Sique', a natural cleft with huge walls of rock on each side about half a mile long and a fantastic defence for the city. Our first sight of the city was the Nabatean-carved beautiful 'rose-red' Treasury. Other buildings are carved into the side of the rock throughout the valley, which also has stone caves with many layers of different colours of sand and small candle-holder niches reminiscent of biblical times.

That evening from the terrace of the hotel we saw the sky ablaze with stars – and many shooting stars. We also went to Jerash – one of the best preserved large Roman cities with a huge amphitheatre, and to Madaba, with a big mosaic map of the Middle East. Mount Nebo was nearby, from where Moses is said to have viewed the Promised Land before the Israelites entered it. Of course we couldn't leave Jordan without visiting the Dead Sea, with its very salty water, in which it was easy to float. However, when a flick of water got into my eye it was most uncomfortable.

In 1993, a 465-page book on *H. pylori*, edited by Stewart and his chief scientist, was published. Thirty-one scientists and doctors from twelve countries – the world experts on *H. pylori* – had responded to Stewart's invitation to contribute to the book; and he wrote the first and last chapters. It was the first work to unite the clinical and biological features of *H. pylori* in one volume.

In the UAE, Stewart and his chief scientist had done research also on brucellosis – spread by the milk of infected goats – and discovered a new 'strain'. In 1995, Stewart received the university prize for all his research, including on antibiotics. He treated his brucellosis patients successfully. When he visited one very rich patient, several relatives and friends were seated around, many with a falcon on their arm, and Stewart was given warm camel milk to drink!

In early 1995, I wrote:

> *Last weekend, with two friends, we were driven in a four-wheel drive through massive oil fields to the interior of the Abu Dhabi Emirate, one hundred and fifty miles from the coast, to go 'roller coasting' up and down the huge (400-500 feet) sand dunes of the Liwa Oasis. For two hundred and fifty years this Oasis had been the simple home base of the ruling family of the Emirate – the Al Nahayans – and no European knew of its existence until 1945! We stopped near the top of a very big dune and saw below us a small oasis of date palms – at the base of a dune. The dew on each dune seeps down to the base, and the moisture collects there; hence the oases. We then were driven what seemed vertically downward to the base of the dune.*

In March, my friend and I accompanied Stewart on his second lecture tour in the Gulf. We started in Bahrain, where we saw Iranian women in traditional black with totally covered faces, and men from Saudi Arabia in their white 'dishdashas' and distinctive headwear. For thousands of years the island of Bahrain had been called Dilmun, and because it was the only area with easy access to wells of drinking water, boats called in there to replenish their supplies. In Doha, Qatar, at that time there was only one hotel! My friend and I found a large, open sandy area, where many men were sitting at small tables, each with a typewriter in front of them. We found someone who could speak English – a young man from Afghanistan with remarkable blue eyes. He told us that the illiterate workers from Pakistan and India were having letters written for them to their families back in their home countries. It was an insight into the culture of the Gulf at that time.

In Kuwait, considering the damage the city sustained during the Gulf War, the restoration programme had been amazing. Flying back to England for our 1991 summer holiday, over Kuwait we had seen the numerous fires of the oil fields set alight by the Iraqis. Fortunately for the country, skilful American oilmen were able put out the fires. It was now four years later. Tourists were not encouraged – it was difficult to get visas – so there was little 'life' in the place. Live music was not allowed, and there is no alcohol. However, there was still a lot of money about, and they are an arrogant people. As a poignant reminder, we saw an Iraqi tank with sand in the wheels in the centre of the main city roundabout. In the souk, traditionally dressed Kuwaiti women from the desert sold their goods, unsupervised by men – unique in a Gulf country.

Then we flew to the far south of Oman, to Salalah, the former capital, which is a more conservative and traditional society than Muscat. In transit we stopped at Muscat airport, where none of the women joining the flight were wearing full veils. These are forbidden in Muscat, but on the plane I was interested to see them covering their faces, so that when they landed in Salalah they were 'appropriately' dressed. The reason why women were forbidden from wearing full veils in Muscat was due to the following incident. A taxi driver was driving two women in his taxi on a very hot day. He noticed that one woman was waving her veil from off their face to get some air – and he was electrified to see that there was a beard underneath the veil! He promptly drove his taxi to the police station and turned the two *men* in. The Sultan of Oman immediately made it a criminal offence in Muscat for any woman to wear a complete veil over their face.

In Salalah, our hotel was on a long, sandy beach, and I watched dolphins sporting in the waves. Meanwhile, my friend accompanied Stewart on a trip inland to the site of the ancient, fabled city of 'Ubar', now the town of Shisur. This had been the source of the frankincense trade for thousands of years up till about 500 A.D.

Frankincense gum requires special climatic conditions for its hard consistency. The trees grow on the escarpment above Salalah, where a sea mist blows in from the ocean but no rain. Thus the trees are slow-growing and hardy, and consequently the sap is thick. The local men make a cut in the trees, and thick sap exudes and hardens, which is frankincense. Shisur was the place where trains of camels started off on their long journey inland, through what is now the Yemen, up to cities in the Middle East and on to Rome, where the frankincense was worth its weight in gold.

Later that year, an expert on fossils from the British Museum came to the UAE and invited our Natural History Group to join him looking for fossils in a remote desert area (Jebel Dhana), where some fossils had been found. Stewart was delighted to go, but the group found only small fossils until the end when the expert was summing up what they had found. Using his shoe, one man started pushing the sand away from what appeared to be a piece of bone. Everyone was astounded when a complete lower jaw of a primitive elephant appeared. This jaw curved downwards, as opposed to current elephants whose lower jaw curves upwards. Nine million years ago, this desert area was well watered and many large animals lived there. It was an exciting find that featured prominently in a subsequent exhibition in the British Museum on the fossils of the UAE.

At Christmas time, I wrote:

> In the autumn, Stewart went to lecture in Japan and converted his business class fare to two economy fares and a week's holiday on the way, for both of us, on Penang Island – 'the Pearl of the Orient'. We felt at home with the strong Chinese element in evidence, and Stewart enjoyed bargaining in Cantonese in the Chinese market stalls and shops. We visited a butterfly farm; the butterflies were fabulous – yellows, blues, greens and reds, some with a six inch wing span. Here in the UAE, Stewart has been most impressed that one of the very wealthy young men, closely related to the ruler, decided to spend seven years studying medicine, when he could have lived a life of luxury. Like all his family, he possessed a string of racing camels – one was the fastest camel in the UAE, worth at least $2 million. He gave a party in the desert for teachers in the Medical School, and before the feast – on a carpet on the sand – the lecturers were invited to take pot-shots with his rifles at targets on a nearby sand-dune.

Before the feast, he excused himself as he said he had another urgent engagement.

In April 1996, a senior Muslim preacher came to speak to the medical students. He had grown up in South Africa aggressively debating with Christian pastors, and knew the Bible very well. He quoted Bible verses that could be interpreted as predicting the arrival of Muhammad rather than Jesus Christ, and he could be very humorous. He had travelled the world widely for many years offering to debate with Christian leaders, but very few were prepared to debate with him. He came to Al Ain, and Stewart sat in the back of the room. Next day some of the students asked Stewart if he would debate in public with this preacher. I said, "No!" but Stewart prayed about it and felt he could talk about the love of God and the Holy Spirit, who is not mentioned in the Koran. So Stewart told the students he would debate – but it was difficult to find a suitable hall for the occasion. Finally, a hall was found and a date arranged. However, in early May, one week before the debate was due, the Muslim preacher had a severe stroke and he never spoke again! The students were very shocked. I was very relieved.

After six and a half years in the UAE, it seemed as though it was time to settle back in England permanently and finally stop our peripatetic life. So in early 1996 Stewart notified the UAE University Medical School that he intended to leave at the end of that academic year, in July. Then I heard that in April there was due to be a trip from the UAE to Yemen, and my friend and I decided to go; but Stewart did not, so as not to use up part of his annual holiday allowance for the academic year 1995-1996. We would get back to England more quickly and avoid the heat. Yemen is very dangerous for foreigners to visit now, and it was beginning to become that way in 1996. So we had to be sure that the country was (relatively) quiet and that we had reliable guides to take us around.

Yemen is one of the oldest civilisations in the Middle East – almost certainly the home of the Queen of Sheba. Sanaa, the capital of Yemen is at an altitude of three thousand feet and is a fascinating place, full of tall buildings with many stories made of granite. In the buildings are coloured glass windows that are such a feature of the country. Our hotel in Sanaa was in one of the tall buildings, and the lozenge-shaped windows cast multicoloured pools on the stone floors,

as the sun shone through the glass. The first evening, my friend and I made a brief exploration out into the narrow streets and saw children playing in a dry, sandy river-bed and many evil-looking dogs barking around. The people all seemed friendly, with the women covered in their long colourful dresses and head scarves. Darkness fell quickly and there were no streetlights, so we made a hurried return to our hotel.

The next morning our group of sixteen met up with our Yemeni guides. There were four Land Rovers, with tough-looking drivers, who each had a Kalashnikov in their vehicle. There had been reports of kidnapping of foreigners, but our chief guide assured us we would be entirely safe with him and his three compatriots. Before I left for Yemen, Stewart told me to always sit behind the driver so that I was not sitting on the edge of the vehicle directly overlooking the various precipices, which seemed to be at the edge of every road! We drove out of Sanaa and headed for the coast.

The Yemenis build their villages on top of tall, steep hills so that they are safe from marauding tribes-people. The residents get their water from streams and rivers at the bottom of the hills, and so there was a steep track up to each village. We stopped and walked up such a track and met a white-haired old man nimbly negotiating the paths with no sign of breathlessness, while we laboured up slowly. Small boys ran up and down the paths like the goats.

We always stopped for a lunch-break at a suitably interesting 'inn'. At one stop, a camel was grinding corn on a stone wheel, round and round. From the mountains, we drove down the escarpment, with spectacular views towards the Red Sea, and passed terraced, well-cared-for fields, but the landscape at sea-level was very different. The small houses were on dry, dusty soil with thorn hedges around them; but it was distressing to see many plastic bags lodged by the wind in the thorn hedges. We stopped on the Red Sea coast at a town called Al Hodeida and saw the thriving fish market. At our night stop slightly farther down the coast it was very hot and humid, and the air-conditioners didn't work. My friend and I decided to try to cool off in the sea, but it was warm and very salty. Further down the coast we went inland to the big city of Taiz and saw fascinating silver jewellery in the large souk. This had been made by a thriving Jewish silversmith community in Yemen, who had now left the country.

Many of the fields are used to grow 'quat'. Its leaf is chewed by Yemeni men every afternoon, as it gives them a 'high'. One day, our driver bought a large quantity for all the drivers but was delayed and then tried to catch up the other vehicles by taking a 'short-cut'. Soon the track narrowed, with a steeper and steeper precipice on the offside, until he realised he could go no further. At that point he said he would turn round. We quickly got out of the vehicle and said, "You can turn round on your own." How he managed to turn the Land Rover around, I don't know. We watched him going backwards and forwards numerous times with his wheels balancing on the edge. Then we all got in again, and he drove back to join the others. If his vehicle had gone over the precipice we would have been left miles from anywhere. Quat is a real problem in the country, as it stops the men working. I feel very privileged to have visited the country, where so few people have gone. Stewart was glad to see me and our friends back safely!

We then began to plan our departure from the UAE. We would be leaving our nice air-conditioned apartment with its incredible views of the sand dunes and camels, and the sunshine and warmth that we had so much enjoyed. Because Al Ain always has a low humidity, we never really found the heat too much. However, it was one thing to say we are going to "settle back in England"; the reality was going to be somewhat different!

CHAPTER TEN

Settling in Wimbledon, and our 40th wedding anniversary.

While were living in the UAE, on one of our usual summer visits back to our flat in Wimbledon, we realised that we would not retire there but would need a house. So in 1993 we spent some time looking at houses we could afford in Wimbledon, and found a town house in a nice cul-de-sac. We rented this out for the last three years we were in the UAE, and when we came back in 1996 to England, we lived there. It had four bedrooms, so there was space for our family to visit us. However, we had not lived in England for any length of time since before 1976!

So we had changed, and of course our home country had changed also. It was a difficult period of adjustment that went on for some time. We found that many local people had never lived anywhere else and seemed uninterested in countries outside Europe or our experiences. However, it was lovely to catch up again with our relatives and friends. We regularly visited my sister Edith in Tunbridge Wells. Grandchildren were born to each of our three married children; and at various times, all our grandchildren stayed with us, and we enjoyed getting to know them and caring for them. We feel it is a great privilege that we have continued to remain in close contact with all our family. We feel blessed to have lived in so many different countries but, above all, to have such a wonderful family whom we continue to appreciate and enjoy.

Travelling had been an essential part of our lives. Up to 1996, we knew 'East of Suez' better than Europe. So we decided that we needed to explore the countries of Europe and were fortunate to be able to take a Danube River cruise from Budapest to the Black Sea. This was

184

extremely interesting and enlightening, stopping at ports in Hungary, Romania and Bulgaria, with trips into these countries that had been under Communist domination.

Our 40th wedding anniversary occurred in 1999, and we invited to the celebration lunch relatives and friends who had been at our wedding. Our children got together and did what they are so very good at doing – organising it all! They decided to buy food from all the different countries we had lived in – Chinese, Indian, Ethiopian, Arabic. It all went wonderfully well.

The family in 2007

EPILOGUE

Looking back is not something I am in the habit of doing, *but* at the end of this account of my life, I realise what an enormous privilege it is to have lived in, not just visited, many different countries. I have learnt something of the culture of the people in each country and the 'ups and downs' of the women I became friends with – their difficulties and joys. It has given me a greater understanding of how to accept people for who they are and the countries from which they come. I am very grateful for the many memories I have of the people I have met and how much they have enriched my journey through life.

However, I remember once saying to my older sister Edith, "Life for me seems to have consisted of saying goodbye!" In my early days by a China sea, I had said goodbye to my sister Patsy who left China in 1940 for higher education in England. Then the Second World War came, and it was six years before I saw her again. Another huge goodbye was when we were driven from our home by the Japanese soldiers when I was only ten years old. This has left me with a sense of loss that surfaces sometimes and a deep sense of the importance of home.

After Stewart and I got married, we followed God's leading to help people physically and spiritually in various countries. So when we went to India and Hong Kong, I had to say goodbye to all my relations and friends, and did not see them again for four years. There was no e-mail in those days and telephoning was too expensive. There were more goodbyes when we went to Ethiopia for two years; then finally in Australia, when each of our children left.

Inevitably, the time that Stewart and I had during the war years in Japanese prisoner of war camps has coloured our lives. I feel fortunate that Stewart and I share this experience. It was amazing that we met up again after the war and then both found ourselves as students in the same London hospital. This led on to our commitment to each other and going overseas in God's service. I am so proud of Stewart's work and research for leprosy patients, and the way he discovered how to detect and reverse nerve damage in these patients – this was a tremendous step forward for such needy people – also, his work in Ethiopia. In Perth, his laboratory work with the bacteria that cause stomach ulcers and stomach cancer has helped numerous patients; and I was fortunate to accompany him to so many countries telling doctors of this discovery.

Working overseas inevitably brings sorrow and unhappiness due to family separations. My mother never had all her six children together with her at one time, partly due to the war. She accepted this but not easily. In China before the war, many Christian workers lived in remote inland areas. When their children came to Chefoo School they might not see their parents for several years because of the difficulties of travelling overland in China at that time; but some parents came to Chefoo in the summer holidays once during a five-year 'term' in China to see them.

The war aggravated this situation, because many parents were working in areas that were not under Japanese occupation. We had many friends from our time in Japanese prison camp who were separated from their parents for five or six years. After the war, this resulted in severe problems in re-establishing family relationships. We met one friend forty years after the war, and when we asked, "What was the most difficult aspect of the separation for you?" she answered, "Meeting my family again after the war!"

Many families who live overseas send their children back to their home countries for boarding school education. This was not something that Stewart and I were prepared to do. We wanted our family always with us, and they have benefited from their experiences of different countries, helping them to become resourceful and independent. However, we are very aware that moving countries, as we have done, has been very disruptive for our family. Losing friends but gaining new ones is never easy. As I finish this book, three of our four children are living in England, and our elder daughter is in New York. I am so grateful to each of them for all their support and encouragement. Without it, I could not have persevered.

Psalm 121, in the Bible, has been a recurring reassurance throughout our lives and during our many upheavals and travels: "The Lord will watch over your coming and going both now and for evermore." So I thank God for all the ways He has led us. Life has often been difficult, but through many trials and difficulties God has been faithful. Thanks be to Him!

Related Books by the Publisher

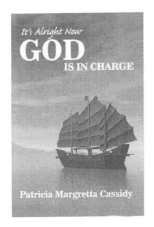

It's Alright Now – God is in Charge
Patricia Margretta Cassidy
ISBN: 978-1-907509-84-1

"There are no Europeans left on the Hill; we should have gone too! Everyone else was evacuated early this morning! We must all go immediately!" The words came tumbling out.

There was no time to argue; it was now known clearly that the Japanese Army had invaded Malaya and was rapidly making its way southwards. In the surrounding area everyone had fled. There was no traffic, no movement anywhere, just silence.

The Second World War and the events that followed shaped Patricia's life as her family travelled from country to country and across three continents. From tigers and bandits to submarines and war camps, the stories of her family highlight the risks, dangers and sufferings experienced in Asia and Africa during that important historical period. Yet we also see how faith in Jesus can guide a family through every trial.

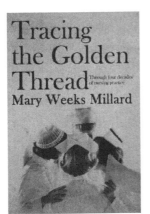

Tracing the Golden Thread
Mary Weeks Millard
ISBN: 978-1-907509-49-0

An inspiring story from the frontline of practical faith in action. Mary Weeks Millard, a quiet and unassuming girl overcomes social shyness and childhood illness and a poor educational start to aspire to her heart's call to become a nurse on the mission field. She tells her own unique and inspiring life story by painting a colourful and often graphic picture of training as a nurse and midwife in the UK in the 1950s. Pressing ahead against all the odds Mary finds doors opening as she exercises her faith in a God of possibilities These doors lead her to adventures and challenges of working in East and Central Africa in the years following independence and civil war before returning to equally challenging situations in UK.